American Foreign Policy

SCOTT FORESMAN PROBLEMS IN AMERICAN HISTORY

*General Editors:* **Edwin Fenton,** *Carnegie Institute of Technology*
**David H. Fowler,** *Carnegie Institute of Technology*

# American Foreign Policy

**Leonard F. James,** *Chairman, Department of History*
*Phillips Academy, Andover, Mass.*

**SCOTT, FORESMAN AND COMPANY**

COVER DESIGN BY ED BEDNO

Library of Congress catalog card #67-12071
Copyright © 1967 by Scott, Foresman and Company, Glenview, Illinois 60025.
All rights reserved.
Printed in the United States of America.
Regional offices of Scott, Foresman and Company are located in
Atlanta, Dallas, Glenview, Palo Alto, and in Oakland, N.J.

6/5/66

Laureat

1.22

# Editors' Introduction

Growing numbers of history teachers realize that using source materials in their courses provides an added dimension of experience for their students. Total reliance on a textbook can no longer be considered an adequate means of learning history. Yet if the full value of documents and critical articles is to be obtained, they must be presented as something more than writings which record important events or as mere illustrations of what the text says. They must also challenge the student's ability to relate individual events to larger topics and to continuing themes in history.

Each volume of the SCOTT FORESMAN PROBLEMS IN AMERICAN HISTORY organizes source materials around one facet of our nation's past. A volume contains fifteen Problems, each designed for one day's work. In some of the books the Problems are intended to be read individually, at the proper chronological intervals. In others, they are grouped into three units of five Problems each, such a unit being best used as an uninterrupted week's work. Whether the Problems are studied individually or in units, they should be assigned only after the student has read the relevant material in his textbook.

One of the most vital services a collection of source materials can perform is to encourage the student to develop his critical abilities to the utmost in constructing historical explanations. Interpretation is the heart of history; the student should be brought to realize how essential it is to be able to do more with facts than memorize them. The SCOTT FORESMAN PROBLEMS are specifically designed to engage the student in the fascinating task of interpreting American history. Through them he will gain the skills and the enjoyment which come from reaching insight and understanding as well as knowledge of history.

Each Problem begins with an introduction written by the author to place documents in their historical context and to link together the Problems in a volume. These introductions prepare the student to read intelligently by defining the scope of the Problem, suggesting its relationship to larger issues, and pointing out difficulties of interpretation so that he will not attempt the impossible in generalizing from limited evidence.

The study questions at the end of the introduction carry the student further in applying the historian's critical tools. He may be asked to try to judge the reliability of a document or the bias of a critic, to assess an historical interpretation in the light of his knowledge, or to reason from particulars to a general conclusion of his own. Properly used, the study questions help beginning students find out what is important in source materials; without them, students often do not know what they are supposed to do with the readings.

To obtain more from a Problem than simply answers to the author's questions, the student should first read the introduction and questions and then pause to review what he already knows about the subject. Then, keeping the central issues in mind, he should study the entire Problem, perhaps first skimming through it to see the relationship of the parts to the whole, and then reading it carefully and taking notes. He will then be ready to consider his answers to the study questions in preparation for class discussion.

The teacher can use the SCOTT FORESMAN PROBLEMS in several ways. A Problem can perhaps serve most effectively as the basis for discussion by an entire class, with the lesson organized around the study questions or other questions proposed by the teacher to develop new points of view. What seems most appropriate for discussion will always depend partly upon the textbook used in the course and partly upon the instructor's own style of teaching and command of the subject. Each teacher should structure the discussion around those issues which he thinks are most important, but he should take care to link a Problem to those which precede and which follow it. These connecting links give the student the maximum opportunity to comprehend the theme of the volume. By treating a limited number of issues within each Problem, a teacher should be able to restrict discussion to one class period.

These volumes can be used in other ways. Many readings can serve as the basis for reports to the class by individual students. An entire volume, or a selection of Problems from a volume, may be used in preparing a controlled research paper; the three-unit volumes are especially suited to this purpose. The Problems may also be assigned as supplementary reading in those areas where text treatment is not extensive.

In *American Foreign Policy* Leonard James directs the student toward discussion of fifteen significant problems in the history of American foreign policy. While each of the problems is presented in its historical context, together they show the continuity as well as the changes in American foreign policies. Understanding how successful—or how faulty—these policies have been in meeting specific situations helps the student analyze international relations and American objectives in foreign policy today. Such analysis encourages him to participate in what James calls "the constant effort to devise intelligent new policies and to effect revisions of outworn ones."

EDWIN FENTON
DAVID H. FOWLER

PUBLISHER'S NOTE: The readings in this volume show capitalization and spelling of words, as well as sentence punctuation, as they appear in the sources from which they were taken. Thus, although the Problem introductions and headnotes are according to Scott, Foresman and Company editorial style, many of the readings are not. Omissions from the original texts are shown by ellipses, and interpolations, supplied by the author or editors for clarity, appear in brackets.

# Table of Contents

# Author's Introduction

From the alliance of the American colonies with France in 1778 to the American interventions in Asia in the twentieth century, the United States government has followed certain basic plans in shaping its relationships with foreign nations. This book examines fifteen examples of the uses of American foreign policy and raises questions which are important to any age in history about the intelligent pursuit of foreign relations.

A foreign policy is a plan by which one nation conducts its relations with other nations. Even if a government should not engage in foreign relations, it still has a foreign policy: isolation. While national foreign policies differ greatly, each includes both a set of objectives (what a nation hopes to achieve through foreign relations) and a set of methods (how that nation means to pursue those goals).

Any nation, in establishing a foreign policy, wants to preserve its own independence and integrity. Closely related to this objective is the one of security for the nation and its citizens. A third goal is prosperity. For some nations at some times, desire for revenge against an enemy or desire for prestige may also be important.

On occasion, nations define specific ideals or ideas as primary objectives. In asking Congress to declare war against Germany in 1917, Woodrow Wilson said, "The world must be made safe for democracy." Soviet leaders declare that the furthering of Communism throughout the world is a primary goal of their nation.

While broad primary objectives such as self-preservation, security, and prosperity tend to guide all nations at all times, the methods for attaining them are likely to differ according to circumstances. For example, circumstances such as the geographical position of a nation may place that nation near to or distant from its enemies or its allies. Military and economic power, ethnic and religious ties, and reactions to international situations differ from nation to nation and from time to time. What was an appropriate policy for the United States when the Atlantic was six weeks wide by sailing ship is not appropriate in a time when that ocean is twenty minutes wide by ballistic missile.

The student must define success or failure of a foreign policy in terms of the historical situation that shaped it. Policy makers never have full freedom of choice. Their alternatives are restricted by preceding events and by existing conditions. Sometimes these alternatives amount to no more than a set of unhappy choices; in that case, policy makers have to choose the least damaging course of action.

In evaluating policies, the student must also consider both short- and long-term effects. For example, Adolph Hitler's foreign policy, aimed at subduing all of Western Europe, was extremely successful until 1941. However, it was unsuccessful in that it led to Hitler's ruinous defeat in World War II and to partition of Germany. Historians may point to the defeat and partition as key elements in the great post-war effort for European cooperation, a movement which would not have occurred when it did without the war. Did Hitler's policy, then, serve the "true" interest of the German people? Most people would say not, but obviously what is defined as "true" interest depends on who is doing the defining.

Understanding how and why American foreign policies have taken shape and what effects they have had is important to all Americans in the constant effort to devise intelligent new policies and to effect revisions of outworn ones.

LEONARD F. JAMES

PROBLEM 1

# The Entangling Alliance of 1778

The American colonies faced defeat in the Revolutionary War unless they could get help from a foreign nation. In 1776 France began to send them modest amounts of secret, unofficial aid. This help was completely unofficial because France could not afford to support the rebellion openly until the colonies showed a good chance of winning their independence. The Americans, vitally aided by French munitions in New Hampshire, won the battle of Saratoga in October 1777. Because of this victory, the French government felt that it could openly support the new government of the United States.

On February 6, 1778 the French recognized the independence of the United States by signing two treaties: one, a commercial agreement and the other, a political and military alliance. By ratifying these treaties on May 4, the United States accepted official French aid and pledged its support if France should become involved in a war with Great Britain. Both France and the United States agreed to neither conclude an armistice or make peace with Great Britain without the consent of the other. The government was willing to undertake the obligations to France because the alliance was necessary to winning the Revolutionary War.

In 1789 the French people overwhelmed the Bourbon monarchy. In attempting to establish a republic, the French won the sympathy of many people in the United States, who saw them as followers of the American example. But, after the execution of Louis XVI in 1793, revolutionary France began an aggressive expansion into neighboring countries, provoking Great Britain to declare war. Many Americans who had sympathized with the French cause disapproved of French actions and did not want to support them. They saw that aggression in Europe could involve the United States, through the Alliance of 1778, in a war with England.

President George Washington expected that France would ask for aid from the United States. Realizing that war would risk independence, Washington tried to determine both the capability of the United States to aid France and the legality of the French request for that aid before he took definite action. How could he deal with the practicalities of war and still maintain enough consistency in foreign policy to preserve the honor of the United States?

As you read, consider the following questions:

1    How did Jefferson and Hamilton differ in their opinions about the validity of the French treaty? Did their ideas about the nature of American interests differ greatly? How?

2    How might these two opinions on a problem in foreign affairs reflect political differences in domestic affairs? Which of the two men seems to have held more faith in the republican form of government?

3    What was Washington's advice on agreements and alliances with foreign nations? Under what conditions can a policy based on this advice be successful?

4    Diplomatic historians have commented that the young United States profited greatly from disagreements among European nations. To what extent was this true in the case of the French alliance?

# I

## AMERICAN INTERESTS vs. GOOD FAITH, 1793

Edmond Genêt was an envoy of the Convention government in France and, thus, represented the radicals who had executed the French king and queen. He landed at Charleston, South Carolina, early in 1793 and journeyed toward Philadelphia, the American capital, to present his credentials to President Washington and to request United States aid against Britain. Genêt was entertained royally along his route through the back country, where sympathizers with the French Revolution were numerous. Washington was perplexed as to what course to follow because receiving Genêt might obligate the United States to honor the Alliance of 1778. The President asked his cabinet for advice in a memorandum dated April 18, 1793. ☐ John C. Fitzpatrick, Editor, *The Writings of George Washington*, Volume 32, pp. 419-420. Washington, D.C.: United States Government Printing Office.

Question I. Shall a proclamation issue for the purpose of preventing interferences of the Citizens of the United States in the War between France and Great Britain &ca.? Shall it contain a declaration of Neutrality or not? What shall it contain?

Questn. II. Shall a Minister from the Republic of France be received?

Quest. III. If received shall it be absolutely or with qualifications; and if with qualifications, of what kind?

Quest. IV. Are the United States obliged by good faith to consider the Treaties heretofore made with France as applying to the present situation of the parties. May they either renounce them, or hold them suspended 'till the Government of France shall be *established*

Questn. V. If they have the right is it expedient to do either, and which?

Questn. VI. If they have an option, would it be a breach of Neutrality to consider the Treaties still in operation?

Quest. VII. If the Treaties are to be considered as now in operation is the Guarantee in the Treaty of Alliance applicable to a defensive war only, or to War either offensive or defensive? . . .

X. What is the effect of a Guarantee such as that to be found in the Treaty of Alliance between the United States and France? . . .

Quest. XII. Should the future Regent of France send a Minister to the United States ought he to be received?

XIII. Is it necessary or advisable to call together the two Houses of Congress with a view to the present posture of European Affairs? If it is, what should be the particular object of such a call?

Thomas Jefferson, Secretary of State, and Alexander Hamilton, Secretary of the Treasury, replied to the President's questions. Characteristic of their feelings on other political issues, Jefferson and Hamilton differed in their opinions on receiving the French minister and honoring the treaties of 1778. The following reading is excerpted from Jefferson's reply. ☐ Paul L. Ford, Editor, *The Writings of Thomas Jefferson*, Volume 6, pp. 220-223, 230-231. New York: G. P. Putnam's Sons, 1895.

I consider the people who constitute a society or nation as the source of all authority in that nation, as free to transact their common concerns by any agents they think proper, to change these agents individually, or the organisation of them in form or function whenever they please: that all the acts done by those agents under the authority of the nation, are the acts of the nation, are obligatory on them, . . . & can in no wise be annulled or affected by any change in the form of the government, or of the persons administering it. Consequently the Treaties between the U. S. and France, were not treaties between the U. S. & Louis Capet [Louis XVI], but between the two nations of America & France, and the nations remaining in existence, tho' both of them have since changed their forms of government, the treaties are not annulled by these changes. . . .

. . . For observe, it is not the *possibility of danger,* which absolves a party from his contract: for that possibility always exists, & in every case. It existed in the present one at the moment of making the contract. . . .

. . . The danger apprehended, is it that, the treaties remaining valid, the clause guarantying their West India islands will engage us in the war? But Does the Guarantee engage us to enter into the war in any event?

Are we to enter into it before we are called on by our allies? Have we been called on by them?—shall we ever be called on? Is it their interest to call on us?

Can they call on us before their islands are invaded, or imminently threatened?

If they can save them themselves, have they a right to call on us?

Are we obliged to go to war at once, without trying peaceable negociations with their enemy?

Are we in a condition to go to war?

Can we be expected to begin before we are in condition?

Will the islands be lost if we do not save them? Have we the means of saving them?

If we cannot save them are we bound to go to war for a desperate object?

. . . But the reception of a Minister from the Republic of France, . . . it is thought will bring us into danger: because this, it is said, will determine the continuance of the treaty, and take from us the right of self-liberation when at any time hereafter our safety would require us to use it. . . .

. . . The Republic of the U. S. allied itself with France when under a despotic government. She changes her government, declares it shall be a Republic, prepares a form of Republic extremely free, and in the mean time is governing herself as such, and it is proposed that America shall declare the treaties void because 'it may say with truth that it would not have allied itself with that nation, if it had been under the present form of it's government!' Who is the American who can say with truth that he would not have allied himself to France if she had been a republic? or that a Republic of any form would be as *disagreeable* as her antient despotism?

Upon the whole I conclude

That the treaties are still binding, notwithstanding the change of government in France: that no part of them, but the clause of guarantee, holds up *danger,* even at a distance. . . .

That the receiving a Minister from France at this time is an act of no significance with respect to the treaties, amounting neither to an admission nor a denial of them.

The following reading is excerpted from Hamilton's reply to Washington. ☐ Henry Cabot Lodge, Editor, *The Works of Alexander Hamilton,* Volume 4, pp. 370-371, 373-376, 385, 393. New York: G. P. Putnam's Sons, copyright 1885.

The treaties between the United States and France were made with His Most Christian Majesty, his heirs and successors. The government of France which existed at the time those treaties were made, gave way, in the first instance, to a new constitution, formed by the representatives of the nation, and accepted by the king, which went into regular operation. Of a sudden a tumultous rising took place. The king was seized, imprisoned, and declared to be suspended by the authority of the National Assembly, a body delegated to exercise the legislative functions of the already established government—in no shape authorized to divest any other of the constituted authorities of its legal capacities or powers. So far, then, what was done was a manifest assumption of power. . . .

The present war, then, turns essentially on the point—What shall be the future government of France? Shall the royal authority be restored in the person of the successor of Louis, or shall a republic be constituted in exclusion of it? . . .

Are the United States bound, by the principles of the laws of nations, to consider the treaties heretofore made with France as in present force and operation between them and the actual governing powers of the French nation? or may they elect to consider their operation as suspended, reserving also a right to judge finally whether any such changes have happened in the political affairs of France as may justify a renunciation of those treaties? . . .

Two nations may form an alliance because each has confidence in the energy and efficacy of the government of the other. A revolution may subject one of them to a different form of government—feeble, fluctuating, and turbulent, liable to provoke wars, and very little fitted to repel them. . . .

The conclusion from the whole is . . . to hold the operation of the treaties suspended; and . . . , if the form of government established in France shall be such as to render a continuance of the treaties contrary to the interests of the United States, they may be renounced. . . .

. . . When all Europe is, or is likely to be, armed in opposition to the authority of the present government of France, would it not be to carry theory to an extreme, to pronounce that the United States are *under* an *absolute,* indispensable obligation, not only to acknowledge respectfully the authority of that government, but to admit the immediate operation of treaties, which would constitute them at once its ally?

# II

## TOWARD AN AMERICAN POLICY, 1796

Washington issued a proclamation of neutrality in April 1793. Although it was loudly opposed, the President's declaration was generally supported by Americans. The French did not demand that the United States participate in the war; they preferred to receive supplies, which slipped through the British blockade on neutral American ships. In 1796, before leaving the presidency, Washington issued a farewell message in which he gave the young American nation advice about its future foreign policy.  ☐ John C. Fitzpatrick, Editor, *The Writings of George Washington,* Volume 35, pp. 231-235. Washington, D.C.: United States Government Printing Office.

Observe good faith and justice towds. all Nations. Cultivate peace and harmony with all. Religion and morality enjoin this conduct; and can it be that good policy does not equally enjoin it? It will be worthy of a free, enlightened, and, at no distant period, a great Nation, to give to mankind the magnanimous and too novel example of a People always guided by an exalted justice and benevolence. . . .

In the execution of such a plan nothing is more essential than that permanent, inveterate antipathies against particular Nations and passionate attachments for others should be excluded; and that in place of them just and amicable feelings towards all should be cultivated. The Nation, which indulges towards another an habitual hatred, or an habitual fondness, is in some degree a slave. It is a slave to its animosity or to its affection, either of which is sufficient to lead it astray from its duty and its interest. . . .

So likewise, a passionate attachment of one Nation for another produces a variety of evils. Sympathy for the favorite nation, facilitating the illusion of an imaginary common interest, in cases where no real common interest exists, . . . betrays the former into a participation in the quarrels and Wars of the latter. . . .

The Great rule of conduct for us, in regard to foreign Nations is in extending our commercial relations to have with them as little *political* connection as possible. So far as we have already formed engagements let them be fulfilled, with perfect good faith. Here let us stop.

Europe has a set of primary interests, which to us have none, or a very remote relation. Hence she must be engaged in frequent controversies, the causes of which are essentially foreign to our concerns. Hence therefore it must be unwise in us to implicate ourselves, by artificial ties, in the ordinary vicissitudes of her politics, or the ordinary combinations and collisions of her friendships, or enmities:

Our detached and distant situation invites and enables us to pursue a different course. If we remain one People, under an efficient government, the period is not far off, when we may defy material injury from external annoyance; when we may take such an attitude as will cause the neutrality we may at any time resolve upon to be scrupulously respected; when belligerent nations, under the impossibility of making acquisitions upon us, will not lightly hazard the giving us provocation; when we may choose peace or war, as our interest guided by our justice shall Counsel.

Why forego the advantages of so peculiar a situation? Why quit our own to stand upon foreign ground? Why, by interweaving our destiny with that of any part of Europe, entangle our peace and prosperity in the toils of European Ambition, Rivalship, Interest, Humour or Caprice?

'Tis our true policy to steer clear of permanent Alliances, with any portion of the foreign world. So far, I mean, as we are now at liberty to do it, for let me not be understood as capable of patronising infidility to existing engagements . . . .

Taking care always to keep ourselves, by suitable establishments, on a respectably defensive posture, we may safely trust to temporary alliances for extraordinary emergencies.

Harmony, liberal intercourse with all Nations, are recommended by policy, humanity and interest.

# III

## ABROGATION OF THE FRENCH TREATIES, 1800

A modern historian described how the United States escaped from the treaties with France.    □  Julius W. Pratt, A History of United States Foreign Policy, pp. 82-84. Englewood Cliffs, New Jersey: Prentice-Hall, Inc., copyright 1955.

France was now (1796) under the rule of the unscrupulous group of politicians known as the Directory. Elated by a series of military victories in Europe, they were reducing the smaller neighbors of France to the role of satellites and tributaries. They proposed to do the same with the United States. Angered by Jay's treaty [U.S. – British commercial treaty, 1794], they refused to receive [Charles Cotesworth] Pinckney [as minister to France], suspended the functions of the French minister in Philadelphia, thereby severing diplomatic relations, ordered French cruisers and privateers to seize American ships (on the theory that what the British could do the French could do), and dabbled in American politics with a view to swinging the election of 1796 in favor of Jefferson and his Republicans and against the Federalist John Adams. Adams (elected nevertheless) named a commission of three—John Marshall, Elbridge Gerry of Rhode Island (a Republican), and the rejected Pinckney—to seek a restoration of diplomatic relations and a promise to respect American rights. Upon their arrival in Paris the commissioners were approached by intermediaries—designated by X, Y, and Z in the printed dispatches—who offered, on behalf of Foreign Minister Talleyrand, recognition by the Directory at the price of a loan to France, a substantial bribe to the Directors, and an apology for some unfriendly references to France in President Adams's recent message to Congress.

The commissioners spurned the proposal. Their report, submitted to Congress by President Adams, with the recommendation that the nation arm itself for defense, stimulated Congress to vigorous action. The lawmakers authorized the President to raise a "provisional army" of

10,000 men in addition to the Regular Army, and called George Washington back from retirement to command it. They created a Navy Department (such small Navy as the United States possessed had hitherto been administered by the Secretary of War) and authorized United States naval vessels and armed merchantmen to attack and capture armed French vessels in the western Atlantic and the Caribbean. And they declared the treaties of 1778 with France abrogated. The Army was not used, though Alexander Hamilton, as senior major general under Washington, would have liked to lead it against Florida and Louisiana, the possessions of Spain, formerly an enemy of France but now her ally. The little Navy gave a good account of itself, capturing between eighty and ninety armed French vessels.

This was the "quasi-war" with France of 1798 to 1800. That it should become a full-scale war was not the desire of President Adams or of Talleyrand, or of General Napoleon Bonaparte, who in November 1799 overthrew the Directory and as First Consul became the head of the French government. Adams, besides being a man of peace, had no wish to see military laurels gathered by his rival, Hamilton. Bonaparte and Talleyrand, now intent upon securing Louisiana, for that reason desired peace with both the United States and Great Britain. Adams, in one of his messages to Congress, had declared that he would never send another minister to France without assurance that he would be "received, respected, and honored as the representative of a great, free, powerful, and independent nation." Talleyrand sent word that a new minister would be thus received and treated. Adams, against the wishes of Secretary of State Timothy Pickering and other members of his cabinet, who wished the undeclared war to continue, named a new commission of three men, William Vans Murray, Oliver Ellsworth, and William R. Davie, to undertake a new negotiation with France.

The American negotiators were received in Paris with all proper respect. They found that Talleyrand, in his desire for a settlement, had already ordered an end to the seizure of American ships and was arranging for the release of captured American sailors. A commission headed by Joseph Bonaparte, the First Consul's brother, was appointed to negotiate with the Americans. Murray and his colleagues asked indemnity for French depredations upon American commerce and bilateral abrogation of the treaties of 1778—already abrogated in so far as an act of Congress could perform that function. The French commissioners pointed out that the claims for indemnity rested upon alleged French violations of the treaty of amity and commerce and said to the American commissioners in effect, "If you wish the indemnity, you must keep the treaties; if you insist upon cancelling the treaties, you must forgo the indemnity." . . . As amended by the Senate and further qualified by Bonaparte before ratification, the treaty nullified the earlier treaties and cancelled the claims for indemnity. Thus the United States escaped from its "entangling alliance" with France—so indispensable during the Revolution, so inconsistent with American interest thereafter. . . .

The chief importance of the treaty of 1800 with France lay in its termination of the treaty of alliance and of the special privileges enjoyed by France under the other [commercial] treaty of 1778. Thus the United States was released from all obligations that compromised its neutral position in relation to the European belligerents.

PROBLEM 2

# Protecting the
# Western Hemisphere

Thomas Jefferson, in his first inaugural address on March 4, 1801, reminded Americans of their favored position of isolation from Europe, "kindly separated by nature and a wide ocean from the exterminating havoc of one quarter of the globe." Jefferson issued a warning against "entangling alliances," emphasizing George Washington's earlier advice against "permanent alliances." American statesmen could avoid interfering directly in European affairs; the difficult question was whether the United States could avoid involvement with European nations which had possessions on American frontiers.

The French Revolution in 1789 and the rise of Napoleon in 1799 undermined monarchies throughout Europe. The ruling families and those people who depended for their positions on the traditional form of government eventually rose against the liberal movements, defeated Napoleon in 1815, and formed alliances to protect their positions. In 1818 Austria, Russia, Prussia, and Britain admitted France to the Quintuple Alliance (popularly called the Holy Alliance); and in 1820 and 1821 these countries repressed rebellions in Spain, Portugal, Naples, and Greece. Britain, not wishing to remain in a league which seemed to have as its main purpose quelling internal popular political revolutions, ceased participating in the Quintuple Alliance in 1822 and took an opposing position. French troops marched into Spain in the spring of 1823 and restored the reactionary Ferdinand VII to the throne later that year. The question which bothered the United States was whether France would assist Ferdinand in recovering control of the Spanish colonies in America, most of which had revolted successfully against the mother country.

A simultaneous extension of European influence into the Western Hemisphere took place on the Pacific coast of North America. There Russia asserted claims to the coastline nearly as far south as the present state of Washington and denied non-Russian ships the right to come within 115 miles of the coast above the fifty-first parallel.

Until this time the efforts of the United States to extend the area of its influence and to ward off potentially hostile forces had been successful. In 1818 the British agreed to the forty-ninth parallel as the northern boundary of the United States west of the Rocky Mountains; helpless Spain ceded Florida to the United States in 1819 and agreed on a generous western boundary for the Louisiana Purchase. Spanish influence in Central and South America diminished between 1808 and 1823 in favor of small republics established through revolutions. However, the threats of French intervention from Mexico and Russian intervention from the northwest continued to make Americans fearful of "the exterminating havoc of one quarter of the globe." How could the United States, unable to muster forces strong enough to wage wars, deter such intervention? As you read, consider the following questions:

**1**   What policy did Jefferson hint at in his letter to Robert R. Livingston? How effective do you think the argument would have been with Napoleon? with the British?

**2**   How would you describe Jefferson's ideas of a favorable situation in Europe, so far as the United States was concerned? Of which nation was he most afraid? Did his attitudes change between 1802 and 1823?

**3**   Why did John Quincy Adams show such an interest in Cuba? What, in effect, was he asking the American minister to tell the Spanish court? Upon what factors would the success of such an American declaration depend?

**4**   What was the chief difference in the advice given Monroe by Jefferson and Adams about Canning's proposal? What were the most important considerations governing Monroe's decision to take an independent stand? How did the Monroe Doctrine guarantee the independence of the new Latin American republics? How did it guarantee American security?

# I

## CHALLENGING AMERICAN SECURITY

Thomas Jefferson argued in a letter to Robert R. Livingston, minister to France, that French possession of the Louisiana Territory and, more especially, occupation of New Orleans would be disadvantageous to the United States. The letter, dated April 1802, arrived in France after Livingston and special emissary James Monroe had agreed to buy the disputed land for $15 million. The first of the following two readings is excerpted from Jefferson's letter to Livingston. □ Paul L. Ford, Editor, *The Writings of Thomas Jefferson*, Volume 8, pp. 144-145. New York: G. P. Putnam's Sons, 1897.

The . . . [cession] of Louisiana and the Floridas by Spain to France works most sorely on the U. S. On this subject the Secretary of State has written to you fully. Yet I cannot forbear recurring to it personally, so deep is the impression it makes in my mind. It compleatly reverses all the political relations of the U. S. and will form a new epoch in our political course. Of all nations of any consideration France is the one which hitherto has offered the fewest points on which we could have any conflict of right, and the most points of a communion of interests. From these causes we have ever looked to her as our *natural friend,* as one with which we never could have an occasion of difference. Her growth therefore we viewed as our own, her misfortunes ours. There is on the globe one single spot, the possessor of which is our natural and habitual enemy. It is New Orleans, through which the produce of three-eighths of our territory must pass to market, and from its fertility it will ere long yield more than half of our whole produce and contain more than half our inhabitants. France placing herself in that door assumes to us the attitude of defiance. . . . [These] circumstances render it impossible that France and the U. S. can continue long friends when they meet in so irritable a position. . . . The day that France takes possession of N. Orleans . . . seals the union of two nations who in conjunction can maintain exclusive possession of the ocean. From that moment we must marry ourselves to the British fleet and nation. We must turn all our attentions to a maritime force, for which our resources place us on very

high grounds. . . . This is not a state of things we seek or desire. It is one
which this measure, if adopted by France, forces on us, as necessarily
as any other cause, by the laws of nature, brings on its necessary effect.
It is not from a fear of France that we deprecate this measure proposed
by her. For however greater her force is than ours compared in the ab-
stract, it is nothing in comparison of ours when to be exerted on our soil.
But it is from a sincere love of peace, and a firm persuasion that bound
to France by the interests and the strong sympathies still existing in the
minds of our citizens, and holding relative positions which ensure their
continuance we are secure of a long course of peace. Whereas the change
of friends, which will be rendered necessary if France changes that position, embarks us necessarily as a belligerent power in the first war of
Europe. In that case France will have held possession of New Orleans
during the interval of a peace, long or short, at the end of which it will
be wrested from her.

The challenge to American security had changed by April 25, 1812, when
Jefferson wrote to James Maury, an old friend in England. In the letter Jefferson
explained why Britain had become a threat to United States interests.   □ Paul
L. Ford, Editor, The Writings of Thomas Jefferson, Volume 9, pp. 348-349.
New York: G. P. Putnam's Sons, 1898.

Our two countries are to be at war, but not you and I. And why
should our two countries be at war, when by peace we can be so much
more useful to one another? Surely the world will acquit our government
from having sought it. Never before has there been an instance of a
nation's bearing so much as we have borne. Two items alone in our cata-
logue of wrongs will forever acquit us of being the aggressors: the im-
pressment of our seamen, and the excluding us from the ocean. . . . I
think the war will not be short, because the object of England, long
obvious, is to claim the ocean as her domain, and to exact transit duties from every vessel traversing it. . . . We consider the overwhelming power of England on the ocean, and of France on the land, as destructive of the prosperity and happiness of the world, and wish both
to be reduced only to the necessity of observing moral duties. We believe no more in Bonaparte's fighting merely for the liberty of the seas,
than in Great Britain's fighting for the liberties of mankind. The object
of both is the same, to draw to themselves the power, the wealth and the
resources of other nations. We resist the enterprises of England first,
because they first come vitally home to us. . . . When the wrongs of

France shall reach us with equal effect, we shall resist them also. But one at a time is enough; and having offered a choice to the champions, England first takes up the gauntlet.

On January 1, 1814, Jefferson wrote to an American friend, Thomas Leiper, and expressed his fear of a Napoleonic Europe. ☐ Paul L. Ford, Editor, *The Writings of Thomas Jefferson*, Volume 9, p. 445. New York: G. P. Putnam's Sons, 1898.

That Bonapart is an unprincipled tyrant, who is deluging the continent of Europe with blood, there is not a human being . . . who does not see: nor can there, I think, be a doubt as to the line we ought to wish drawn between his successes and those of Alexander. Surely none of us wish to see Bonaparte conquer Russia, and lay thus at his feet the whole continent of Europe. This done, England would be but a breakfast; and, though I am free from the visionary fears which the votaries of England have affected to entertain, because I believe he cannot effect the conquest of Europe; yet put all Europe into his hands, and he might spare such a force to be sent in British ships, as I would as leave not have to encounter, when I see how much trouble a handful of British soldiers in Canada has given us. No. It cannot be to our interest that all Europe should be reduced to a single monarchy. The true line of interest for us, is, that Bonaparte should be able to effect the complete exclusion of England from the whole continent of Europe.

Expressing his feelings in the spring of 1823, Secretary of State John Quincy Adams was convinced that Britain was more of a threat to the United States than either Spain or France. ☐ Worthington Chauncey Ford, Editor, *Writings of John Quincy Adams*, Volume 7, pp. 370, 372, 374, 379, 381. New York: The Macmillan Company. Copyright 1917 by Mary Ogden Adams.

It has been a maxim in the policy of these United States, from the time when their independence was achieved, to keep themselves aloof from the political systems and contentions of Europe. To this principle it is yet the purpose of the President to adhere . . . .
. . . [It] may be taken for granted that the dominion of Spain upon the American continents, North and South, is irrecoverably gone. But the islands of Cuba and of Porto Rico still remain nominally and so far really dependent upon her, that she yet possesses the power of transferring her own dominion over them, together with the possession of

them, to others. These islands, from their local position, are natural appendages to the North American continent . . . .

. . . As Spanish territory the island [Cuba] will be liable to invasion from France during the war: and the only reasons for doubting whether the attempt will be made are the probable incompetency of the French maritime force to effect the conquest, and the probability that its accomplishment would be resisted by Great Britain. . . .

The transfer of Cuba to Great Britain would be an event unpropitious to the interests of this Union. . . . The question both of our right and our power to prevent it, if necessary, by force, already obtrudes itself upon our councils, and the administration is called upon, in the performance of its duties to the nation, at least to use all the means within its competency to guard against and forefend it. . . .

You will not conceal from the Spanish government the repugnance of the United States to the transfer of the island of Cuba by Spain to any other power. . . . [That] the condition of Cuba cannot be changed without affecting in an eminent degree the welfare of this Union, and consequently the good understanding between us and Spain; that we should consider an attempt to transfer the island, against the will of its inhabitants, as subversive of their rights, no less than of our interests; and that, as it would give them the perfect right of resisting such transfer, by declaring their own independence, so if they should, under those circumstances, resort to that measure, the United States will be fully justified in supporting them to carry it into effect.

# II

## FORMULATING A POLICY

By 1822 British merchants had gained commercial predominance in the former Spanish colonies of America. British Foreign Secretary George Canning thought that France might cooperate with Ferdinand VII of Spain in reasserting Spanish power in Latin America. Canning sent a note to Richard Rush, United States minister to Great Britain, in August 1823, proposing a joint British-American agreement to resist such action. Rush replied to Canning in warm but noncommittal fashion and referred the message to his superiors in Washington. The following reading is excerpted from Canning's proposal. ☐ William R. Manning, Editor, *Diplomatic Correspondence of the United States Concerning the Independence of the Latin-American Nations*, Volume 3, p. 1478. New York: Oxford University Press and Carnegie Endowment for International Peace, copyright 1925.

Is not the moment come when our Governments might understand each other as to the Spanish American Colonies? And if we can arrive at such an understanding, would it not be expedient for ourselves, and beneficial for all the world, that the principles of it should be clearly settled and plainly avowed?

For ourselves we have no disguise.

1. We conceive the recovery of the Colonies by Spain to be hopeless.
2. We conceive the question of the Recognition of them, as Independent States, to be one of time and circumstances. . . .
4. We aim not at the possession of any portion of them ourselves.
5. We could not see any portion of them transferred to any other Power, with indifference.

If these opinions and feelings are as I firmly believe them to be, common to your Government with ours, why should we hesitate mutually to confide them to each other; and to declare them in the face of the world?

President Monroe was aware that Canning's note presented an opportunity to establish a new American policy. In evaluating that opportunity, Monroe asked for the opinions of former President Jefferson and Secretary of State John Quincy Adams. In a letter dated October 24, 1823, Jefferson encouraged the President to accept Canning's proposal. The following excerpt is from Jefferson's reply. □ Paul L. Ford, Editor, The Writings of Thomas Jefferson, Volume 10, pp. 277-279. New York: G. P. Putnam's Sons, 1899.

The question presented by the letters you have sent me, is the most momentous which has ever been offered to my contemplation since that of Independence. . . . Our first and fundamental maxim should be, never to entangle ourselves in the broils of Europe. Our second, never to suffer Europe to intermeddle with . . . affairs [on this side of the Atlantic]. America, North and South, has a set of interests distinct from those of Europe, and peculiarly her own. She should therefore have a system of her own, separate and apart from that of Europe. . . . One nation, most of all, could disturb us in this pursuit; she now offers to lead, aid, and accompany us in it. By acceding to her proposition, we detach her from the bands, bring her mighty weight into the scale of free government, and emancipate a continent at one stroke . . . . Great Britain is the nation which can do us the most harm of any one, or all on earth; and with her on our side we need not fear the whole world. With her then, we should most sedulously cherish a cordial friendship; and nothing would tend more to knit our affections than to be fighting once more, side by side, in the same cause. Not that I would purchase even her amity at the price of taking part in her wars. But the war in which the present proposition might engage us, should that be its consequence, is not her war, but ours. Its object is to introduce and establish the American system, of keeping out of our land all foreign powers, of never permitting those of Europe to intermeddle with the affairs of our nations. It is to maintain our own principle, not to depart from it. And if . . . we can effect a division in the body of the European powers, and draw [Great Britain] over to our side . . . , surely we should do it. . . .

. . . I should think it, therefore, advisable, that the Executive should encourage the British government to a continuance in the dispositions expressed in these letters.

The following reading is a portion of Adams' diary notation of November 7, 1823. □ Charles Francis Adams, Editor, *Memoirs of John Quincy Adams*, Volume 6, pp. 177-179. Philadelphia: J. B. Lippincott & Co., copyright 1875.

We have no intention of seizing either Texas or Cuba. But the inhabitants of either or both may exercise their primitive rights, and solicit a union with us. They will certainly do no such thing to Great Britain. By joining with her, therefore, in her proposed declaration, we give her a substantial and perhaps inconvenient pledge against ourselves, and really obtain nothing in return. Without entering now into the enquiry of the expediency of our annexing Texas or Cuba to our Union, we should at least keep ourselves free to act as emergencies may arise, and not tie ourselves down to any principle which might immediately afterwards be brought to bear against ourselves. . . .

. . . It would be more candid, as well as more dignified, to avow our principles explicitly to Russia and France, than to come in as a cock-boat in the wake of the British man-of-war.

# III

## THE MONROE DOCTRINE

Adams' advice was incorporated into President Monroe's annual message to Congress in December 1823. By the time Monroe made his declaration, the threat of British interference had thwarted European intervention; and the United States stood secure without committing itself to Canning's proposal. France had assured Britain that it did not intend to intervene in America and

Russia had decided to withdraw from its position in the Pacific Northwest. The significance of the Monroe Doctrine is that it established a standard for policy which American national consciousness would one day be able to accept and which American power would one day be able to enforce. Excerpts from Monroe's message follow. ☐ James D. Richardson, Compiler, *Messages and Papers of the Presidents, 1789-1897*, Volume 2, p. 218. Washington, D.C.: Authority of Congress. Copyright 1897 by James D. Richardson.

In the wars of the European powers in matters relating to themselves we have never taken any part, nor does it comport with our policy so to do. It is only when our rights are invaded or seriously menaced that we resent injuries or make preparation for our defense. With the movements in this hemisphere we are of necessity more immediately connected, and by causes which must be obvious to all enlightened and impartial observers. The political system of the allied powers is essentially different in this respect from that of America. . . . We owe it, therefore, to candor and to the amicable relations existing between the United States and those powers to declare that we should consider any attempt on their part to extend their system to any portion of this hemisphere as dangerous to our peace and safety. With the existing colonies or dependencies of any European power we have not interfered and shall not interfere. But with the Governments who have declared their independence and maintained it, and whose independence we have, on great consideration and on just principles, acknowledged, we could not view any interposition for the purpose of oppressing them, or controlling in any other manner their destiny, by any European power in any other light than as the manifestation of an unfriendly disposition toward the United States.

PROBLEM 3

Continental Expansion

Between 1846 and 1848 the United States fought a war with comparatively helpless Mexico, gaining, as a result, land which comprises the states of California, Nevada, Utah, New Mexico, and Arizona. Some men feared expansion as a new opening for slavery, but most Americans welcomed the addition of territory. Of those people who approved the results of the Mexican War, many questioned the use of military force in achieving them. Was the war justified by the need for more land?

Expansion west of Missouri attracted little interest among Americans before 1830 because of a belief that the land, called the "Great American Desert," was too dry for development. Emigration of American nationals beyond the western boundary of the United States began in earnest in the 1830's with the establishment of Stephen Austin's colony in the lush grasslands of Texas. Illinois and Iowa frontiersmen moved to the Pacific Northwest when "Oregon fever" struck them in 1842. Brigham Young's Mormon community settled near the Great Salt Lake in 1847. The successful development of these communities proved that men could live in the West and helped dispel the myth of the Great American Desert.

Americans were encouraged in their expansion by a belief, popular especially after 1845, that it was their "manifest destiny" to dominate the continent. This domination was seen as a moral mission to extend the benefits of democracy. In the presidential campaign of 1844, the Democratic candidate, James K. Polk, won the election with the promise that he would annex Texas, an independent republic since 1836, and Oregon, held jointly by the United States and Britain. Polk also intended to acquire California from Mexico if the opportunity arose. President John Tyler succeeded in having Congress vote to annex Texas only a few days before Polk assumed office. Because Mexico had never recognized Texan independence, Tyler's action caused Mexico to break diplomatic relations with the United States and doomed Polk's efforts for peaceful expansion.

After an unsuccessful attempt to buy California, Polk ordered American troops into the area between the Nueces and Rio Grande rivers, claimed by both Mexico and the United States. He later ordered General Zachary Taylor to move his troops south to the Rio Grande. Mexican forces retaliated by attacking a company of American cavalry. Because sixteen Americans were killed or wounded in this skirmish, it furnished the occasion for the declaration of war which Polk had been preparing. The successes of the Mexican War, together with an agreement with the British in 1846 over Oregon, gave the United States full control over nearly all its transcontinental domain.

As you read, consider the following questions:

1    Do you find any statements in the several excerpts which indicate that a moral principle motivated the war?

2    Do you think that national security justified the war with Mexico? Why?

3    Did Latané and Ferrell have any point of agreement about justification for the war? On what do they disagree?

4    Do you think that there were any justifications for the Mexican War? Was it, to use a modern term, an "imperialistic" war?

# I

**POLK DEFENDS HIS POLICY TOWARD MEXICO**

Learning early in 1846 that the Mexican government refused to discuss territorial questions with Commissioner John Slidell, President Polk ordered American forces to the Rio Grande River. On May 9 he attempted to convince his cabinet that declaring war was justified, and when the cabinet learned of the Mexican attack on an American cavalry detachment, every member concurred. In his message to Congress on May 11, the President asked for a declaration of war. ☐ James D. Richardson, Compiler, *Messages and Papers of the Presidents, 1789-1897*, Volume 4, pp. 482-483, 488. Washington, D.C.: Authority of Congress. Copyright 1897 by James D. Richardson.

[There] are those who, conceding . . . [that Texas was independent], assume the ground that the true western boundary of Texas is the Nueces instead of the Rio Grande, and that therefore in marching our Army to the east bank of the latter river we passed the Texan line and invaded the territory of Mexico. A simple statement of facts known to exist will conclusively refute such an assumption. Texas, as ceded to the United States by France in 1803, has been always claimed as extending west to the Rio Grande or Rio Bravo. . . . Down to the conclusion of the Florida treaty, in February, 1819, by which this territory was ceded to Spain, the United States asserted and maintained their territorial rights to this extent. . . .

The Texas which was ceded to Spain by the Florida treaty of 1819 embraced all the country now claimed by the State of Texas between the Nueces and the Rio Grande. The Republic of Texas always claimed this river as her western boundary, and in her treaty made with Santa Anna in May, 1836, he recognized it as such. By the constitution which Texas adopted in March, 1836, senatorial and representative districts were organized extending west of the Nueces. The Congress of Texas on the 19th of December, 1836, passed "An act to define the boundaries of the Republic of Texas," in which they declared the Rio Grande from its mouth to its source to be their boundary, and by the said act they extended their "civil and political jurisdiction" over the country up to that boundary. . . .

After the joint resolution for the annexation of Texas to the United States had been passed by our Congress the Mexican minister at Washington addressed a note to the Secretary of State, bearing date on the 6th of March, 1845, protesting against it as "an act of aggression the most unjust which can be found recorded in the annals of modern history, namely, that of despoiling a friendly nation like Mexico of a considerable portion of her territory," and protesting against the resolution of annexation as being an act "whereby the Province of Texas, an integral portion of the Mexican territory, is agreed and admitted into the American Union;" and he announced that as a consequence his mission to the

United States had terminated, and demanded his passports, which were granted. It was upon the absurd pretext, made by Mexico (herself indebted for her independence to a successful revolution), that the Republic of Texas still continued to be, notwithstanding all that had passed, a Province of Mexico that this step was taken by the Mexican minister.

Every honorable effort has been used by me to avoid the war which followed, but all have proved vain.

# II

## WHIG OPPONENTS OF WAR CRITICIZE POLK

While thousands of volunteers rushed to enlist in the Army, the Mexican War was by no means popular throughout the United States. Many Whigs bitterly opposed President Polk's declaration of war. The opinions of Congressman Abraham Lincoln from Illinois were expressed in a speech before the House of Representatives on January 12, 1848. □ Roy P. Basler, Editor, *The Collected Works of Abraham Lincoln,* Volume 1, pp. 433-434. New Brunswick, New Jersey: Rutgers University Press. Copyright 1953 by The Abraham Lincoln Association of Springfield, Illinois.

The President, in his first war message of May 1846, declares that the soil was *ours* on which hostilities were commenced by Mexico; and he repeats that declaration, almost in the same language, in each successive annual message, thus showing that he esteems that point, a highly essential one. In the importance of the point, I entirely agree with the President. To my judgment, it is the *very point,* upon which he should be justified, or condemned. In his message of Decr. 1846, it seems to have occurred to him, as is certainly true, that title—ownership—to soil, or any thing else, is not a simple fact; but is a conclusion following one or more simple facts; and that it was incumbent upon him, to present the facts, from which he concluded, the soil was ours, on which the first blood of the war was shed. . . .

. . . Now I propose to try to show, that the whole of this,—issue and evidence—is, from beginning to end, the sheerest deception. The issue, as he presents it, is in these words "But there are those who, conceding all this to be true, assume the ground that the true western boundary of Texas is the Nueces, instead of the Rio Grande; and that, therefore, in marching our army to the east bank of the latter river, we passed the Texan line, and invaded the territory of Mexico." Now this issue, is made up of two affirmatives and no negative. The main deception of it is, that it assumes as true that *one* river or the *other* is necessarily the boundary; and cheats the superficial thinker entirely out of the idea, that *possibly* the boundary is somewhere *between* the two, and not actually at either. A further deception is, that it will let in *evidence,* which a true issue would exclude. A true issue, made by the President, would be about as follows "I say, the soil *was ours,* on which the first blood was shed; there are those who say it was not."

I now proceed to examine the President's evidence, as applicable to such an issue. When that evidence is analized, it is all included in the following propositions: . . .

His first item is, that the Rio Grande was the Western boundary of Louisiana, as we purchased it of France in 1803; and . . . that by the treaty of 1819, we sold to Spain the whole country from the Rio Grande eastward, to the Sabine. Now, admitting for the present, that the Rio Grande, was the boundary of Louisiana, what, under heaven, had that to do with the *present* boundary between us and Mexico? How, Mr. Chairman, the line, that once divided your land from mine, can *still* be the boundary between us, *after* I have sold my land to you, is, to me, beyond all comprehension. . . . His next piece of evidence is that "The Republic of Texas always *claimed* this river (Rio Grande) as her western boundary [.]" That is not true, in fact. Texas *has* claimed it, but she has not *always* claimed it. There is, at least, one distinguished exception. Her state constitution,—the republic's most solemn, and well considered act—that which may, without impropriety, be called her last will and testament . . . —makes no such claim. But suppose she had always claimed it. Has not Mexico always claimed the contrary? so that there is but *claim* against *claim,* leaving nothing proved, until we get back of the claims, and find which has the better *foundation.*

Thomas Corwin, Whig Senator from Ohio, also opposed Polk's reasons for going to war.  ☐  Thomas Corwin, Speech made in the Senate, February 11, 1847. Washington, D.C.: *Appendix to the Congressional Globe,* 29th Congress, 2nd Session, Volume 16, pp. 213, 216-217.

I looked to the President's account of it, and he tells me it was a war for the defense of the territory of the United States. I found it written in that message, Mr. President, that this war was not sought nor forced upon Mexico *by the people* of the United States. . . . Sir, I know that the *people* of the United States neither sought nor forced Mexico into this war, and yet I know that the President of the United States, with the command of your standing army, did seek that war, and that *he* forced war upon Mexico. . . .

What is the territory, Mr. President, which you propose to wrest from Mexico? It is consecrated to the heart of the Mexican by many a well-fought battle with his old Castilian master. His Bunker Hills, and Saratogas, and Yorktowns are there! The Mexican can say, "There I bled for liberty! and shall I surrender that consecrated home of my affections to the Anglo-Saxon invaders? What do they want with it? . . . The Senator from Michigan [Mr. Cass] says he must have this. Why, my worthy Christian brother, on what principle of justice? "I want room!"

Sir, look at this pretence of want of room. With twenty millions of people, you have about one thousand millions of acres of land, inviting settlement by every conceivable argument, bringing them down to a quarter of a dollar an acre, and allowing every man to squat where he pleases. But the Senator from Michigan says we will be two hundred millions in a few years, and we want room. If I were a Mexican I would tell you, "Have you not room in your own country to bury your dead men? If you come into mine, we will greet you with bloody hands, and welcome you to hospitable graves." . . .

. . . We want California. What for? Why, says the Senator from Michigan, we will have it; and the Senator from South Carolina [Mr. Calhoun], with a very mistaken view, I think, of policy, says you can't keep our people from going there. . . . Let them go and seek their happiness in whatever country or clime it pleases them. All I ask of them is, not to require this Government to protect them with that banner consecrated to war waged for principles — eternal, enduring truth.

# III

## MODERN HISTORIANS CONSIDER POLK AND THE WAR

Many twentieth-century historians have had mixed feelings about the Mexican War. In 1935, Richard R. Stenberg discussed the attitudes which Polk held toward Texas and the boundary question during the year before the outbreak of war. Portions of Stenberg's article constitute the following reading.
□ Richard R. Stenberg, "The Failure of Polk's Mexican War Intrigue of 1845." Glendale, California: *Pacific Historical Review*, Volume 4, Number 1, March 1, 1935, pp. 40-43.

   Mexico severed relations with the United States in March, 1845, when Congress passed the Texas annexation measure; and uttered threats to reconquer the "lost department." But all this proved mere "sound and fury," for she acquiesced in the annexation, desiring only to save appearances and protect her right to her territory west of the Nueces, to which Texas had no right either legally or by conquest. It suited Polk to declare after war began that hostilities were commenced by Mexico because of annexation—a convenient fiction hardly plausible then and long since exploded. Yet in a certain way the annexation did lead to the war: Polk gave pledges to Texas, when trying to induce her to accept annexation, that he would maintain her claim to the Rio Grande, and in his fulfillment of this (by military occupation, or conquest, instead of by peaceable negotiation, as Congress had intended) he provoked the War with Mexico. . . .

   . . . After his inauguration Polk similarly gave pledges to Texas to do many good things for her if she would accept annexation—pledges which likewise he made no effort afterwards to fulfill, save only that to uphold the Texas paper-claim to the Rio Grande. This last significant pledge placed him in an unpleasant dilemma. Texas claimed to the Rio Grande, though she had never extended west of the Nueces; and the advanced Democratic expansionists had seemingly endorsed the claim at the Baltimore Convention (May, 1844) by demanding the "reannexa- tion" of Texas, a most irrelevant expression historically. But the Whigs and a strong section of the Democracy led by [Missouri Senator Thomas Hart] Benton and holding the balance of power in the Senate held that the Nueces, and not the Rio Grande, was the western boundary of Texas. If Polk should fail to uphold the Texas claim he would anger the Texans and many of his own countrymen; if he upheld it he would be forced to aggress against Mexico—unless (which was very doubtful) she could be bought off or brought peacefully to acquiesce . . . .

   A word, therefore, as to Polk's aims: these were such as war only could fulfill (for it was impossible to suppose that Mexico would will- ingly dismember herself). Polk on taking office in March, 1845, [stated] that the acquisition of California was one of the chief measures he would endeavor to accomplish. In this he could expect the approval of his countrymen: expansive talk of "manifest destiny"—a term coined in 1845—was rife, and predictions assigned the whole continent to the ambitious Americans, who were now moving in ever-increasing numbers into California and Oregon . . . . There were fearsome reports in 1844- 45 that "grasping" England was about to gain California peaceably from

Mexico. At the time the Slidell mission was conceived Polk records in his *Diary* his determination to take New Mexico and California by war if Mexico should refuse to yield a minimum of territory—that east of the Rio Grande—to satisfy private American claims against Mexico. Such evidence is eloquent of Polk's imperialistic desires.

John H. Latané considered the relationship of California to the war crisis. ☐ John Holladay Latané and David W. Wainhouse, *A History of American Foreign Policy,* Second Revision, pp. 264-266. Garden City, New York: The Odyssey Press, Inc., copyright 1940.

The instructions [to Slidell] in regard to California were premised on the statement that, "From information possessed by this department, it is to be seriously apprehended that both Great Britain and France have designs upon California." It was true that both Great Britain and France were pressing Mexico for the payment of the claims of their subjects, that Mexico had recognized these claims and agreed to pay them, but had defaulted, and that there were constant rumors of proposals to satisfy these claims by land cessions in California. Few persons at all familiar with the situation believed that California would long continue a dependency of Mexico, and the general belief was that it would fall either to England or to the United States. In fact, the Mexican government had little authority over the province and, as a British consul wrote to his government, it was "at the mercy of whoever may choose to take possession of it." British residents of California and British naval officers on the Pacific station had long urged their government to acquire the province, but Great Britain was at this time singularly indifferent to colonial expansion, and . . . instructed . . . agents in California to remain entirely passive in the event of an insurrection against Mexico. . . .

The soundness of Polk's apprehensions as to the possibility of California being offered to some European power is confirmed by the fact that in May, 1846, just on the eve of war with the United States, the president of Mexico offered to transfer California to Great Britain in return for a loan. The offer reached England just after a change of ministry, but [Foreign Secretary] Palmerston, who had returned to the foreign office, did not reverse . . . [British] policy. The acceptance of the offer at that time would in fact have been equivalent to a declaration of war against the United States. . . .

The view has been too often taken by American historians that Polk forced war upon Mexico in order that he might have an excuse for taking California. An impartial examination of the documents and other evidence in the case does not warrant such a conclusion. In fact, it was quite evident to most observers, European as well as American, that if peace continued California would in a few years be controlled by emigrants from the United States who would bring the province into the Union after the manner of Texas.

Robert H. Ferrell questioned whether the Mexican War was a just conflict. ☐ Abridgment of pages 106-108. Reprinted from *American Diplomacy, A History* by Robert H. Ferrell. By permission of W. W. Norton & Company, Inc. Copyright © 1959 by W. W. Norton & Company, Inc.

What could one say about manifest destiny, as it had found fulfillment in the events of 1845-1848? The peaceful process by which the United States of America had been expanding across the enormously valuable North American continent had been punctuated by a short and sharp and altogether victorious war. . . . Should not the United States in 1846-1848 have trusted to its diplomacy and restrained its pursuit of manifest destiny, if that were possible?

The answer to this question is not easy. . . .

If Texas had been allowed to go her own way in 1845, if the American government had continued timid and unresponsive to Texan requests for annexation there might have developed another large North American republic between the United States and Mexico. If the manifest destiny of the American people had received this blow there might have followed an independent California on the Pacific Coast, perhaps an independent Oregon. The North American continent, already split south of the Rio Grande into half a dozen or more weak governments, would have gone the way of South America. . . .

. . . The question remains as to whether the Mexican War was a just conflict—whether Americans should in good conscience have avoided the war by which their country took New Mexico and California from a weak Latin government, whether manifest destiny offered only an excuse for a land-hungry nation.

Americans may as well admit that in 1846-1848 they fought a war of aggression against Mexico. Such a confession is discomforting to make in the aggression-ridden twentieth century, but the facts of the case substantiate it. President Polk touched off the war when he ordered General Taylor to the line of the Rio Grande. He hoped to provoke the Mexicans and managed to do it. The war was an act of aggression by the

United States for the purpose of conquering territory from a helpless neighbor. Mexico had little chance of defending herself. . . . Americans, surveying the Mexican War, can argue that their country brought order and prosperity to the regions it conquered, and especially that for the preservation of democracy in the twentieth century this nineteenth-century war was a fortunate affair. Such argument does not alter the fact that the method employed in 1846-1848 to extend American sovereignty westward to the Pacific was aggression and that the war against Mexico was not a just war.

This statement of fact, however, does not dispose of the justification for the war, manifest destiny, the mystic notion that the North American continent was destined to belong to the people of the United States. As one examines the course of Mexican-American relations in the early nineteenth century it does seem that, apart from the rightness or wrongness of the Mexican War, there was an undeniable logic in United States possession of Texas, New Mexico, and California. One has therefore the uneasy feeling that the result of the war was good but the means were bad, and that perhaps if the American people in 1846-1848 had been possessed of more wisdom they would have found another method, besides war—presumably a correct diplomatic method—by which to realize their good end, their manifest destiny.

PROBLEM 4

# Acquiring the Philippines

Although the United States restricted its expansion to the North American continent throughout the nineteenth century, some Americans interpreted the principle of "manifest destiny" as a justification for vigorous expansion across the seas. In 1854 a treaty of annexation was negotiated with Hawaii but never signed. In 1878 and 1884 the United States obtained coaling stations at Pago-Pago in Samoa and Pearl Harbor in Hawaii. The Republican platform of 1896 advocated the annexation of Hawaii, the building of a Nicaraguan canal, and the purchase of the Danish West Indies.

American relations with Cuba, also guided by the principle of "manifest destiny," eventually led to war with Spain and the acceptance of a colonial empire by the United States. Cuba, a colony of Spain, had been of concern to the United States ever since other Latin-American colonies had rebelled against the mother country in the early nineteenth century. United States policy makers feared that a revolt of the Cubans against Spain might lead to the kind of foreign intervention which would threaten United States interests. James K. Polk offered to buy the island in 1848, and in 1852 the British and French governments proposed to the

United States a joint declaration that all three "disclaim, now and here-after, all intention to obtain possession of Cuba." The United States rejected the proposal, stating that Cuba was an American question. In 1854 the United States offered Spain $130 million for Cuba, but Spain rejected the offer.

When revolution broke out in Cuba in 1868, with charges of atrocities on both sides, the United States maintained strict neutrality. In 1895, however, the United States responded to another rebellion by issuing a sharp protest to Spain on the grounds of inhumanity and injustice. After the sinking of the U.S.S. *Maine* in February 1898, President William McKinley appealed to the Spanish government to stop removing Cuban natives from the countryside into areas behind Spanish lines, to stop the fighting, and to agree not to resume the fighting after Cuba was granted independence. McKinley, under intense public pressure to force Spain out of Cuba, virtually ignored concessions made by Spain and demanded Cuban independence. When Spain refused to comply in full with McKinley's ultimatum, it accepted war with the United States.

During the Spanish-American War, the United States gained control of the Philippine Islands and Guam in the Pacific as well as Puerto Rico and Cuba in the Caribbean. Bowing to both the anti-imperialists and the American sugar producers who feared unrestricted Cuban competition, the President granted limited independence to Cuba shortly after the termination of the three-months war. The United States had two alternatives with regard to the Philippines, Guam, and Puerto Rico: one was to maintain the islands as colonial possessions and the other choice was to abandon them to the designs of European powers. McKinley's decision to retain control of the island empire led to a re-definition of national interests and responsibilities.

As you read, consider the following questions:

1    What kinds of Americans probably would have approved of Josiah Strong's *Our Country?* What kinds would have disapproved? Why would they have approved or disapproved?

2    How would the excerpts in Reading 2 have appealed to American business interests? to humanitarian attitudes?

3    How did Bryan apply the term "imperialism" to the acquisition of Spanish territories? Do you think that Bryan used the term correctly? Why?

4    How did Lodge's justification for the acquisition of the Philippines constitute a reversal of traditional United States policy?

**5** Do you think that there was a better way for McKinley to settle the fate of the Philippines than by assuming control of them?

# I

## THE IDEA OF MISSION

Josiah Strong, author, lecturer, and minister, used Charles Darwin's theory of evolution to support his belief that people of Anglo-Saxon ancestry enjoyed a social and moral superiority over other people. He saw this superiority as a divine commission to the Anglo-Saxons to rule all the nations of the world. □ Josiah Strong, *Our Country*, pp. 208, 210, 214, 218, 221-223, 226-227. New York: The American Home Missionary Society, copyright 1891.

The Anglo-Saxon is the representative of two great ideas, which are closely related. One of them is that of civil liberty. Nearly all of the civil liberty of the world is enjoyed by Anglo-Saxons: the English, the British colonists, and the people of the United States. . . .

The other great idea of which the Anglo-Saxon is the exponent is that of a pure *spiritual* Christianity. . . . Without controversy, these are the forces which, in the past, have contributed most to the elevation of the human race, and they must continue to be, in the future, the most efficient ministers to its progress. It follows, then, that the Anglo-Saxon, as the great representative of these two ideas, the depositary of these two greatest blessings, sustains peculiar relations to the world's future, is divinely commissioned to be, in a peculiar sense, his brother's keeper. . . .

There can be no reasonable doubt that North America is to be the great home of the Anglo-Saxon, the principal seat of his power, the center of his life and influence. . . .

Mr. Darwin . . . says: "There is apparently much truth in the belief that the wonderful progress of the United States, as well as the character of the people, are the results of natural selection . . .".

Again, another marked characteristic of the Anglo-Saxon is what may be called an instinct or genius for colonizing. His unequaled energy, his indomitable perseverance, and his personal independence, made him a pioneer. He excels all others in pushing his way into new countries. . . .

. . . There are no more new worlds. The unoccupied arable lands of the earth are limited, and will soon be taken. The time is coming when the pressure of population on the means of subsistence will be felt here as it is now felt in Europe and Asia. Then will the world enter upon a new stage of its history—*the final competition of races, for which the Anglo-Saxon is being schooled.* Long before the thousand millions are here, the mighty *centrifugal* tendency, inherent in this stock and strengthened in the United States, will assert itself. Then this race of unequaled energy . . . will spread itself over the earth. If I read not amiss, this powerful race will move down upon Mexico, down upon Central and South America, out upon the islands of the sea, over upon Africa and beyond. And can any one doubt that the result of this competition of races will be the "survival of the fittest?" . . .

In my own mind, there is no doubt that the Anglo-Saxon is to exercise the commanding influence in the world's future . . . . We of this generation and nation occupy the Gibraltar of the ages which commands the world's future.

# II

## AMERICAN ATTITUDES TOWARD CUBA

The American protest to Spain in 1895 was a recognition of growing interest in expansion, and the question of intervention in Cuba was debated in Congress many times before the Spanish-American War. The first of the following two excerpts is from a speech made in 1896 by Republican Senator Henry Cabot Lodge of Massachusetts. ☐ *Congressional Record*, 54th Congress, 1st Session, February 20, 1896, p. 1972.

The great island lies there across the Gulf of Mexico. She commands the Gulf, she commands the channel through which all our coastwise traffic between the Gulf and our Northern and Eastern States passes. She lies right athwart the line which leads to the Nicaragua Canal. Cuba in our hands or in friendly hands, in the hands of its own people, attached to us by ties of interest and gratitude, is a bulwark to the commerce, to the safety, and to the peace of the United States.

We should never suffer Cuba to pass from the hands of Spain to any other European power. We may dismiss that aspect of the subject. The question is whether we shall permit the present condition of affairs to continue. The island to-day is lost to Spain. They may maintain a guerrilla warfare for years. . . .

Recognition of belligerency as an expression of sympathy is all very well. I think it is fully justified by the facts in Cuba, but I should like to see some more positive action taken than that. I think we can not escape the responsibility which is so near to us. We can not shrug our shoulders and pass by on the other side. If that war goes on in Cuba, with the added horrors which this new general brings with him, the responsibility is on us; we can not escape it. We should exert every influence of the United States. Standing, as I believe the United States stands, for humanity and civilization, we should exercise every influence of our great country to put a stop to that war which is now raging in Cuba and give to that island once more peace, liberty, and independence.

Republican Senator George Louis Wellington of Maryland believed that a declaration favoring the belligerency of the insurgents in Cuba would lead to war with Spain. In May 1897 he urged the Senate not to become involved in the Cuban revolution. □ *Congressional Record*, 55th Congress, 1st Session, May 17, 1897, pp. 1089, 1091.

Our first duty is to the American people, not to Cuba, not as against Spain, not with respect to Turkey or England or any foreign nation. It is to the American people that the Senate of the United States owes present, aye, immediate, attention. . . .

Where is the civil government upon the Island of Cuba? Where is the capital of the government? Where is the congress that is there assembled? Where are the legislatures? Where is the president of the republic? Where is its judiciary? Where the many things that would denominate and demonstrate the fact that there is in Cuba to-day a civil government? Nowhere. They exist only in the imagination of those who are carried away by sentiment and sympathy. I do not believe that sentiment should guide this nation in its foreign policy. I would have my country stand by international law and follow the path of severe justice and national advancement. But if it is to be a matter of sentiment, then, sir, there is sentiment upon the other side. . . .

Make haste slowly. You do not know what may follow. This is a defiance to Spain by reason of the dangerous situation it creates. You may say Spain is a weak power; that Spain can be demolished and annihilated by our forces in thirty minutes, as has been suggested in the newspapers. I doubt it. Are you ready for war? Ask the general of your Army; ask the commander of your Navy. Is the American Republic ready for war? I do not believe it is. If one of the great nations of Europe were to come here to-day, they could demolish every port you have on the Atlantic coast . . . before you could gather strength to prevent or resist an invasion.

# III

## THE DEBATE OVER THE PHILIPPINES

Because he was under severe criticism for his decision to control the Philippines, President McKinley tried to justify his action. Portions of his statement constitute the following reading. □ Charles S. Olcott, *William McKinley,* Volume 2, pp. 110-111. Boston: Houghton Mifflin Company. Copyright 1916 by Charles S. Olcott.

I have been criticized a good deal about the Philippines, but don't deserve it. The truth is I didn't want the Philippines, and when they came to us, as a gift from the gods, I did not know what to do with them. When the Spanish War broke out, Dewey was at Hong-kong, and I ordered him to go to Manila and to capture or destroy the Spanish fleet, and he had to; because, if defeated, he had no place to refit on that side of the globe, and if the Dons were victorious, they would likely cross the Pacific and ravage our Oregon and California coasts. And so he had to destroy the Spanish fleet, and did it! But that was as far as I thought then.

When next I realized that the Philippines had dropped into our laps I confess I did not know what to do with them. I sought counsel from all sides . . . but got little help. I thought first we would take only Manila; then Luzon; then other islands, perhaps, also. I walked the floor of the White House night after night until midnight; and I am not ashamed to tell you, gentlemen, that I went down on my knees and prayed Almighty God for light and guidance more than one night. And one night late it came to me this way—I don't know how it was, but it came: (1) That we could not give them back to Spain—that would be cowardly and dishonorable; (2) that we could not turn them over to France or Germany—our commercial rivals in the Orient—that would be bad business and discreditable; (3) that we could not leave them to themselves—they were unfit for self-government—and they would soon have anarchy and misrule over there worse than Spain's was; and (4) that there was nothing left for us to do but to take them all, and to educate the Filipinos, and uplift and civilize and Christianize them, and by God's grace do the very best we could by them, as our fellow

48

men for whom Christ also died. And then I went to bed, and went to sleep, and slept soundly, and the next morning I sent for the chief engineer of the War Department (our map-maker), and I told him to put the Philippines on the map of the United States [pointing to a large map on the wall of his office], and there they are, and there they will stay while I am President!

The two excerpts which follow are from speeches made by William Jennings Bryan in 1899. In them he discussed the acquisition of a colonial empire and explained why he had questioned McKinley's action. ☐ William J. Bryan, "The Savannah Interview." *The Second Battle*, pp. 87-88. Chicago: W. B. Conkey Company, copyright 1900.

I may be in error, but in my judgment our nation is in greater danger just now than Cuba. Our people defended Cuba against foreign arms; now they must defend themselves and their country against a foreign idea—the colonial idea of European nations. . . . Our nation must give up any intention of entering upon a colonial policy, such as is now pursued by European countries, or it must abandon the doctrine that governments derive their just powers from the consent of the governed.

. . . Paraphrasing Lincoln's declaration, I may add that this nation cannot endure half republic and half colony—half free and half vassal. Our form of government, our traditions, our present interests and our future welfare, all forbid our entering upon a career of conquest.

☐ William J. Bryan, "America's Mission." *The Second Battle*, pp. 107-108, 112-113. Chicago: W. B. Conkey Company, copyright 1900.

When the advocates of imperialism find it impossible to reconcile a colonial policy with the principles of our government or with the canons of morality; when they are unable to defend it upon the ground of religious duty or pecuniary profit, they fall back in helpless despair upon the assertion that it is destiny. . . .

The people have not voted for imperialism; no national convention has declared for it; no Congress has passed upon it. . . .

We have reached another crisis. The ancient doctrine of imperialism, banished from our land more than a century ago, has recrossed the Atlantic and challenged democracy to mortal combat upon American soil. . . .

Anglo-Saxon civilization has taught the individual to protect his own rights, American civilization will teach him to respect the rights of others.

Anglo-Saxon civilization has taught the individual to take care of himself, American civilization, proclaiming the equality of all before the law, will teach him that his own highest good requires the observance of the commandment: "Thou shalt love thy neighbor as thyself."

Anglo-Saxon civilization has, by force of arms, applied the art of government to other races for the benefit of Anglo-Saxons, American civilization will, by the influence of example, excite in other races a desire for self-government and a determination to secure it.

Anglo-Saxon civilization has carried its flag to every clime and defended it with forts and garrisons. American civilization will imprint its flag upon the hearts of all who long for freedom.

Senator Lodge defended McKinley when he spoke of the righteousness of the American position in the Philippines. ☐ *Congressional Record,* 56th Congress, 1st Session, March 7, 1900, pp. 2618, 2627-2629.

I believe we are in the Philippines as righteously as we are there rightfully and legally. I believe that to abandon the islands, or to leave them now, would be a wrong to humanity, a dereliction of duty, a base betrayal of the Filipinos who have supported us . . . .

Our opponents put forward as their chief objection that we have robbed these people of their liberty and have taken them and hold them in defiance of the doctrine of the Declaration of Independence in regard to the consent of the governed. As to liberty, they have never had it, and have none now, except when we give it to them protected by the flag and the armies of the United States. . . .

. . . In a policy which gives us a foothold in the East, which will open a new market in the Philippines, and enable us to increase our commerce with China, I see great advantages to all our people, and more especially to our farmers and our workingmen. . . .

We are also told that the possession of these islands brings a great responsibility upon us. This, Mr. President, I freely admit. A great nation must have great responsibilities. It is one of the penalties of greatness. . . .

. . . There can be no doubt that the islands in our peaceful possession would take from us a very large proportion of their imports. . . . They require railroads everywhere. Those railroads would be planned by American engineers, the rails and the bridges would come from American mills, the locomotives and cars from American workshops. . . .

. . . The Empire of China has a population of . . . over four hundred millions. . . . The work of opening up the country by railroads and of developing its still untouched natural resources has begun and is advancing with giant strides. . . .

. . . We know well that China is threatened by Russia, and that Russian dominion, if unrestrained, would mean discrimination and exclusion in the Chinese markets. . . . The possession of the Philippines made us an Eastern power, with the right and, what was equally important, the force behind the right to speak. . . . A policy which proposes to open wider markets . . . requires that we should save the teeming millions of China from . . . [Russia], and keep them free, not merely for the incoming of commerce, but for the entrance of the light of Western civilization, seems to me a great and noble policy, if there ever was such, and one which may well engage the best aspirations and the highest abilities of American statesmanship.

# IV

## WHY DID THE UNITED STATES KEEP THE PHILIPPINES?

Samuel Flagg Bemis, well-known diplomatic historian, commented on the issues and personalities which involved the United States in colonial responsibilities following the Spanish-American War. ☐ Samuel Flagg Bemis, A Diplomatic History of the United States, pp. 468-469, 471. New York: Holt, Rinehart and Winston, Inc., copyright 1953.

The great question therefore remaining before President McKinley and his advisers was whether to keep any or all of the Philippines. They were confronted squarely with the issue of outright and undisguised imperialism. This was the most important question in foreign policy which the nation had been called upon to decide since its independence. An absolutely new question, it had to be decided promptly in the fever-time of exuberant war feeling. President Washington a century before had warned his countrymen not to involve themselves in European political questions. The Monroe Doctrine had laid down such abstention as a fundamental principle of American foreign policy. Should the United States now involve itself at once in both European and Asiatic political questions, as it must needs do if it took over the Philippines, assuming vast liabilities in a part of the world where its interests were not vital, treading a political labyrinth where its step was least secure and its vision least luminous? Should it choose the perilous path of imperialism in the Far East, amid lands and peoples so distant from the American system and so alien to it?

Before the war there had not been the slightest demand for the acquisition of the Philippine Islands. The average American citizen could not have told you whether Filipinos were Far Eastern aborigines or a species of tropical nuts. . . . But the expansionists of 1898, the new imperialists, the Roosevelts, the Lodges, the Mahans, the exponents of a "large" policy, knew where the Philippines were and they soon wanted them for the United States . . . . In his annual message of 1897 President McKinley had stated, anent Cuba, that forcible annexation was unthinkable — "that, by our code of morality, would be criminal aggression." This did not prevent him from thinking of annexation of other islands once the war began. "While we are conducting war and until its conclusion," he noted, "we must keep all we get; when the war is over we must keep what we want." What did the country want?

In the last analysis it is President McKinley who must bear the responsibility of the acquisition of the Philippines, as well as of the war with Spain, for it is he who commanded the army and navy, and who dictated the instructions to the American plenipotentiaries at [the treaty talks in] Paris.

PROBLEM 5

The Open Door in China

The United States, committed to the control of the Philippine Islands, assumed increasing interest in the Far East after 1898. At the same time, however, it was reluctant to take an official position on questions concerning the problems of the Chinese Empire. With the Open Door policy, Secretary of State John Hay tried to reconcile the differences between the expansionists, who wanted the United States to assume responsibility as a world leader, and the traditionalists, who wanted it to maintain a policy of non-alignment.

The authority of the Chinese government was seriously weakened when, in the Sino-Japanese War of 1894-1895, Japan defeated China and obtained control of Korea. Seeing that the leaders of China were unable to resist foreign intervention, France, Britain, Germany, and Russia gained concessions called "spheres of influence" from them.

Britain, with a large economic stake in China, thought that if partition could not be prevented, the next best arrangement would be a free and fair system of economic opportunity for all nations in all areas of China. The British government proposed that any Chinese territory taken by a foreign power should be declared "open to all on precisely similar conditions." The United States refused to cooperate with Britain in this joint effort to guarantee an "open door" in China. However, Secretary Hay proposed an open door policy in a memorandum sent on September 6, 1899, to American representatives in Berlin, London, and St. Petersburg. He later sent similar notes to Rome, Tokyo, and Paris. Although five powers replied to the proposal in conditional terms and Russia remained silent, Hay announced that all six powers had indicated their agreement to it.

Beginning in the fall of 1898, local militia units, created by the government of China as a reserve peace force, began to be recruited from among men who were accustomed to lives of violence. Intensely patriotic and anti-foreign, these men came to be known by the English as the Boxers. Throughout 1899 the Boxers organized anti-foreign demonstrations and riots, and in June 1900 the Chinese government declared war on the Western powers, citing persistent aggressions on China as justification.

On July 3, 1900 foreign troops were attempting to relieve their legations in Peking, which had been beseiged by the Boxers. At that time, Hay sent another note to the six powers, stating the American policy toward China. The first note guaranteed the territorial integrity of China only on the condition that other powers would do the same; but the second note declared that the United States would make that guarantee, whether or not other nations wanted to do the same. Since no one nation trusted the others, each one indicated that it would follow the example of the United States, although the statements were generally vague.

The nature of the Open Door policy and its significance to the position of the United States in Asia have been matters of great interest and controversy. There is little doubt, for example, that the protective attitude manifested by the United States toward China after 1900 played a part in arousing Japanese animosity in the years before the Pearl Harbor attack in 1941.

As you read, consider the following questions:

1    Would you define the "Open Door" as (a) the purpose (justification) of a foreign policy, or (b) the method (plan) of a policy?

2    Why did Quincy, Lippmann, and Halle think that the United States adopted the Open Door policy? Which man, do you think, is most nearly correct in his assessment of the situation?

3    Do you think that the Open Door policy was a departure from traditional United States policy? How did it indicate a re-evaluation

of the American position in foreign affairs? How did it reflect the traditional attitude?

**4** Do you think that American interference in the Chinese problem was to the best advantage of the United States? If not, do you think that the United States should have adopted a stronger or a weaker policy? Why?

# I

## OPEN DOOR CORRESPONDENCE

The letters which follow show the development of the Open Door policy; they are representative of the correspondence between the United States and those six nations which had or were seeking spheres of influence in China. The first letter, sent to Henry White, Ambassador to Germany, by John Hay on September 6, 1899, was the proposal. ☐ House Documents, *Papers Relating to the Foreign Policy of the United States*, 1899, pp. 129-130. Washington, D.C.: Government Printing Office.

Sir: At the time when the Government of the United States was informed by that of Germany that it had leased from His Majesty the Emperor of China the port of Kiao-chao and the adjacent territory in the province of Shantung, assurances were given to the ambassador of the United States at Berlin by the Imperial German minister for foreign affairs that the rights and privileges insured by treaties with China to citizens of the United States would not thereby suffer or be in anywise impaired within the area over which Germany had thus obtained control.

More recently, however, the British Government recognized by a formal agreement with Germany the exclusive right of the latter country to enjoy in said leased area [the port of Kiao-chao] and the contiguous "sphere of influence or interest" certain privileges, more especially those relating to railroads and mining enterprises . . . .

. . . [The] Government of the United States would be pleased to see His German Majesty's Government . . . lend its cooperation in securing like assurances from the other interested powers, that each, within its respective sphere of whatever influence—

First. Will in no way interfere with any treaty port or any vested interest within any so-called "sphere of interest" or leased territory it may have in China.

Second. That the Chinese treaty tariff of the time being shall apply to all merchandise landed or shipped to all such ports as are within said "sphere of interest" (unless they be "free ports"), no matter to what nationality it may belong, and that duties so leviable shall be collected by the Chinese Government.

Third. That it will levy no higher harbor dues on vessels of another nationality frequenting any port in such "sphere" than shall be levied on vessels of its own nationality, and no higher railroad charges over lines built, controlled, or operated within its "sphere" on merchandise belonging to citizens or subjects of other nationalities transported through such "sphere" than shall be levied on similar merchandise belonging to its own nationals transported over equal distances.

The second letter, sent to White by German Secretary of State for Foreign Affairs Count Bernhard von Bülow on February 19, 1900, was the German reply. ☐ House Documents, *Papers Relating to the Foreign Policy of the United States*, 1899, p. 131. Washington, D.C.: Government Printing Office.

Mr. Ambassador: Your excellency informed me, in a memorandum presented on the 24th of last month, that the Government of the United States of America had received satisfactory written replies from all the powers to which an inquiry had been addressed . . . in regard to the policy of the open door in China. While referring to this, your excellency thereupon expressed the wish that the Imperial Government would now also give its answer in writing. . . .

Gladly complying with this wish, I have the honor to inform your excellency . . . the Imperial Government has, from the beginning, not only asserted, but also practically carried out to the fullest extent, in its Chinese possession, absolute equality of treatment of all nations with regard to trade, navigation and commerce. The Imperial Government entertains no thought of departing in the future from this principle . . . . If, therefore, the other powers interested in the industrial development of the Chinese Empire are willing to recognize the same principles, this can only be desired by the Imperial Government.

The third letter, dated March 20, 1900, announced the agreement of all six nations; it was sent by the United States, with the appropriate insertions, to American representatives in each of the six capitals. ☐ House Documents, *Papers Relating to the Foreign Policy of the United States*, 1899, p. 142. Washington, D.C.: Government Printing Office.

Sir: The _____ Government having accepted the declaration suggested by the United States concerning foreign trade in China, the terms of which I transmitted to you in my instruction No. _____ of _____, and like action having been taken by all the various powers having leased territory or so-called "spheres of interest" in the Chinese Empire, as shown by the notes which I herewith transmit to you, you will please inform the Government to which you are accredited that the condition originally attached to its acceptance—that all other powers concerned should likewise accept the proposals of the United States—having been complied with, this Government will therefore consider the assent given to it by [the appropriate government] as final and definitive.

You will also transmit to the minister for foreign affairs copies of the present inclosures, and by the same occasion convey to him the expression of the sincere gratification which the President feels.

The fourth letter, dated July 3, 1900, was the commitment by the United States to protection of the integrity of China. It was sent to French Ambassador to Washington, Thiébaut, by Secretary Hay. ☐ House Documents, *Papers Relating to the Foreign Policy of the United States,* 1900, pp. 318-319. Washington, D.C: Government Printing Office.

Sir: I have the honor to acknowledge the receipt of your note of yesterday's date . . . .

My conversation with you will have enabled you to see that the policy and attitude of this Government, as already determined by the President, are substantially in the line of the views entertained by the Government of the French Republic. Following the precedents enunciated by the United States as early as 1857, this Government aims at the conservation of peace and amity with the Chinese nation, the furtherance of lawful commerce, and the protection of the lives and interests of American citizens in every part of China by all the means guaranteed under extraterritorial treaty rights and by the law of nations, to which ends we are prepared to uphold the efforts of the Chinese authorities in the provinces to use their powers to protect foreign life and property against the attacks of subversive anarchy, and are resolved to hold to the uttermost accountability the responsible authors of any wrong done to our citizens. To attain these objects the Government of the United States is now, as heretofore, ready to act concurrently with the other powers in opening up communication with Pekin and rescuing the imperiled Americans and foreigners there, to afford all possible protection everywhere in China to American life and property, to guard all legitimate American interests in the Empire, and to aid in preventing a spread of the disorders to other provinces, and in securing future immunity from a recurrence of such disasters—seeking to these ends a solution which may bring about permanent peace and safety to China, preserve Chinese territorial and administrative entity, protect all rights guaranteed to friendly powers by treaty, and safeguard for the world the principle of equal and impartial trade with all parts of the Chinese Empire.

I am communicating these views to all the governments represented diplomatically at Pekin, substantially as herein outlined; and it gives me much pleasure to advise you of their purport, in view of their virtual accord with the policy independently formulated by the Government of the French Republic.

Meanwhile, . . . instructions have been telegraphed to the commander of the United States naval forces in Chinese waters to confer with his colleagues and report as to the force necessary to accomplish the ends now purposed and the proportionate force to be appropriately employed by the United States for their attainment in the general interest of the powers concerned.

# II

## THE NATURE OF THE OPEN DOOR

Josiah P. Quincy, American author and historian, wrote in October 1900 to show how the Open Door was a conservative policy. He believed that it was a good policy because it did not commit the United States to any specific action. ☐ Josiah Quincy, "China and Russia." New York: *North American Review*, Volume 171, Number 527, October 1900, pp. 529-530, 534-535.

The action of our own Government for the last year in connection with Chinese affairs, beginning with the circular note of Secretary Hay relative to the "open door" policy, in September, 1899, has certainly, in the main, been wise and conservative, and it may well be conceded that if the record closes equally well, a creditable chapter will have been added to the annals of American diplomacy. But the critical period of the real difficulties is just upon us, and this may last even for years before any final settlement is effected . . . .

In . . . declaring it to be the policy of the United States to seek a solution of the existing troubles which should "prevent a recurrence of such disasters, bring about permanent safety and peace in China," Secretary Hay plainly implied the intention of our Government to join in political action for the radical reconstruction of Chinese administration. Fortunately, his language is general and does not hold us to any specific programme, and when it suits our convenience we can dismiss it as a mere expression of pious good will toward the Chinese people . . . .

We should never lose sight of the cardinal fact in the Chinese situation, so far as we are concerned—namely, that we have no present or prospective territorial or political interests, "spheres of influence," or "leases" of ports, in China, and that we do not want any—in which respects we are in a radically different position from all the other Powers represented in the concert. If we have joined with other nations in forcing our missionaries and our trade on China, we have not, at least, participated in the exaction of those cessions of territory and comprehensive privileges which seem to have been the direct cause of the present outbreak [the Boxer Rebellion]. We may, therefore, well leave the main task of quelling the storm to those Powers which have raised it, merely safeguarding our own special interests, so far as that is possible. . . .

. . . Fortunately for the United States, in spite of our large army in the Philippines and our troops now in China, no sane American thinks that we will fight with any other member of the concert, whatever may be our policy or our interests, either to prevent the dismemberment of China or to secure any share in the partition for ourselves, or to reform the Chinese government, or even to maintain the "open door" for our trade. This certainly affords another cogent consideration in favor of keeping out of the threatening complications which may lead to war between the Powers; for, if we do not mean to fight, neither do we want to suffer any loss of dignity or prestige.

In the following excerpt, Walter Lippmann explained the Open Door as a popular policy. He argued that the policy was an outgrowth of the American political tradition. □ Copyright 1944, by Walter Lippmann. From *U.S. War Aims* by Walter Lippmann, by permission of Atlantic-Little, Brown and Company.

[From] the earliest days we have contended for an Open Door, so that American traders would have the same commercial rights as those of any other nation. . . . [The] policy of the Open Door is as old as our relations with Asia, . . . it was not limited to China, but was upheld also for Japan and Korea, and on the coast of Africa as early as 1832.

The ardor with which Americans have espoused this principle is the heart of the mystery. The importance to the American people of the whole Oriental trade was, as we have seen, small. The merchants and the investors directly concerned in it could have done fully as well for themselves, probably much better, by entering into combinations with other nations for the colonial exploitation of China. During the past generation, certainly, Japan would have been only too pleased to take the United States into a business partnership, provided we assented to her political domination of China. Had profits been the determining motive, Americans could have had them without the risks of war.

Yet, with deviations from the main line of our principles, which were soon corrected, Americans preached the Open Door incessantly to the other nations, and whenever the Chinese asserted their own independence, we gave them moral and material support. It is evident that the Open Door meant something more to Americans than a commercial policy, and that the missionary zeal with which we have propagated it touches chords of memory and of faith, and is somehow the expression of the American political religion.

The explanation is not far to seek. The American nation was born in a rebellion by the colonists against the mercantilist empire of Great Britain. The Open Door is simply a short name to describe American opposition to the trade monopolies and privileges of the mercantilist system. In the struggle for independence the American people acquired an indelible antipathy to monopolies and privileges established by imperial rule. Thus Americans react by long tradition, which is now well-nigh instinctive, against colonial imperialism. When they have themselves acquired colonies, as in the Philippines, they could not rest until they had promised the colonies independence; they were glad to provide the means by which the colonies could achieve independence; and the great majority were pleased when Congress, yielding to the pressure of the sugar lobby and the like, fixed a definite date for Philippine independence.

The American antipathy to imperialism is not a humanitarian sentiment acquired in some casual way. It is organic in the American character, and is transmitted on American soil to all whose minds are molded by the American tradition. It is a deep and pervasive habit of thought because it comes directly from the original conflict in which the colonists became Americans. That explains the missionary zeal with which Americans have championed what is apparently a merely commercial policy.

On the face of it, one may well ask, even today, why they [the Open Door notes] should be regarded as a turning point in the history of our policy. They represented no radical departure from our position, merely the generalizing of it in the form of the "Open Door" proposal to the partitioning powers. However, once the "Open Door" notes had been sent, and replies to them received, they were publicized as an achievement of our diplomacy, they were theatrically identified with American morality in opposition to Old World chicanery, and the American electorate was encouraged to take a magnified view of them in connection with the 1900 elections. The McKinley administration was tempted to present itself to the voters as one that had, in the name of a newly arisen America, brought the slinking dogs of European imperialism to heel in Asia. It did not resist the temptation.

Here was a demonstration, to be repeated at every crisis in the following half century, of the disposition among our people to support foreign policies only when they are presented in the guise of great principles. Defense merely of our own commercial rights in China had no such appeal as the "Open Door" for all nations. . . .

The fact is that . . . [the] "Open Door" policy, so far from frustrating the imperialistic designs of the powers on China, represented the acceptance of China's partitioning. It did not seek guarantees from the government of China but, rather, from the governments of the powers that were replacing Chinese authority with their own. . . .

So the policy of the United States was made. The Notes were sent out, and the powers, momentarily glancing aside from their struggles to maintain or upset the balance of power, made polite replies that were chiefly designed to prevent any appearance that they were not on the side of the angels. The administration, in its public treatment of these replies, gave the impression that the powers would not have been on the side of the angels had it not been for its action in recalling them to the paths of moral duty. Hay appears to have had few illusions about what the replies really meant. . . .

Only a few months after we had announced to the great powers our policy of supporting the integrity of China the Russians virtually grabbed

China's richest province, Manchuria, and made it their own. "I take it for granted," Secretary Hay wrote to President Theodore Roosevelt, "that Russia knows as we do that we will not fight over Manchuria, for the simple reason that we cannot." When Russia refused to get out of Manchuria in deference to our policy, Hay wrote the President: "I am sure you will think it is out of the question that we should adopt any scheme of concerted action with England and Japan. Public opinion in this country would not support such a course, nor do I think it would be to our permanent advantage . . ." Here we see the persistence of the dogma of "no entangling alliances" in an altered situation to which it no longer had any relevance. . . .

What Hay did elicited public praise. Therefore, he and his successors were tempted to do it again and again, each time to the applause of the electorate. So we embarked and continued on the road to Pearl Harbor.

PROBLEM 6

Policy for the Caribbean

In 1823 the United States announced the Monroe Doctrine and thus closed the Western Hemisphere to future European colonization. Unhampered by outside interference, United States citizens began to settle in Oregon and California during the 1840's. Consequently, interest in building a Central American canal, linking Americans on the Atlantic and Pacific coasts, began to grow. After the acquisition of the Philippine Islands in 1898, the desirability of such a canal became even more apparent.

By the Clayton-Bulwer Treaty of 1850 the United States and Britain had agreed that neither nation would exercise exclusive control over or fortify an isthmian canal. In the Hay-Pauncefote Treaty of 1901, however, Britain surrendered its advantage and gave the United States the exclusive right to build, control, and fortify such a canal. The change in policy was influenced by the fact that British supremacy on the sea was threatened by expansion of the German navy, and Britain needed American help in facing such a threat.

The United States tried both to preserve the inviolability of the Western Hemisphere and to guarantee its own preëminence in the Caribbean with the Monroe Doctrine and the Hay-Pauncefote Treaty. But, because of political and economic weaknesses in Latin American nations, European investors began to lose considerable amounts of money; and because the European nations had guaranteed the investments of their citizens, they tried to recover them by assuming control of customs houses in those countries where they had suffered losses.

President Theodore Roosevelt felt that, by using force to resolve the issues, Europeans had challenged the Monroe Doctrine; and he countered with a new policy of active intervention by the United States when Latin American countries were unable to fulfill their obligations to other nations. This policy became known as the Roosevelt Corollary to the Monroe Doctrine. It was strongly criticized by many people who thought that the new policy was as much a threat to Latin American independence as European actions had been.

As you read, consider the following questions:

1    What was the situation which provoked the United States to adopt the Roosevelt Corollary?

2    Did the Monroe Doctrine justify United States interference in the internal affairs of independent Latin American nations? Why do you think so?

3    Did the point of view of the Drago Doctrine conflict with that of Mahan? Did it conflict with the point of view expressed in the Monroe Doctrine? How was it different from the Roosevelt Corollary?

4    What was the significance of the protest by Quintanilla?

5    What course of action could a great power follow toward an underdeveloped nation which would satisfy both the demands of the great power for financial responsibility and political stability and the desire of the underdeveloped nation for true national sovereignty?

# I

## AMERICAN INTERESTS IN THE CARIBBEAN

Writing just before the turn of the twentieth century, Captain Alfred Thayer Mahan, speaking for the importance of naval power, influenced the attitudes of North Americans on foreign affairs. Because United States citizens held important economic interests outside the nation, he encouraged the maintenance of a strong navy to protect those interests.    □ A. T. Mahan, *The Interest of America in Sea Power*, pp. 3-7, 20-21. Boston: Little Brown, and Company, copyright 1897.

For the past quarter of a century, the predominant idea, which has asserted itself... at the polls and shaped the course of the government, has been to preserve the home market for the home industries....

For nearly the lifetime of a generation... American industries have been... protected, until the practice has assumed the force of a tradition, and is clothed in the mail of conservatism....

At bottom, however, the temperament of the American people is essentially alien to such a sluggish attitude. Independently of all bias for or against protection, it is safe to predict that, when the opportunities for gain abroad are understood, the course of the American enterprise will cleave a channel by which to reach them....

The interesting and significant feature of this changing attitude is the turning of the eyes outward, instead of inward only, to seek the welfare of the country. To affirm the importance of distant markets, and the relation to them of our own immense powers of production, implies logically the recognition of the link that joins the products and the markets—that is, the carrying trade; the three together constituting that chain of maritime power to which Great Britain owes her wealth and greatness....

Coincident with... signs of change in our own policy there is a restlessness in the world at large which is deeply significant, if not ominous.... [The] great seaboard powers... do not stand on guard against their continental rivals only; they cherish also aspirations for commercial extension, for colonies, and for influence in distant regions, which may bring, and, even under our present contracted policy, already have brought them into collision with ourselves....

...Europe has now little mercantile interest in the Caribbean Sea. When the Isthmus is pierced, this isolation will pass away, and with it the indifference of foreign nations.... [All] ships that use the canal will pass through the Caribbean.... [The] effect produced upon the prosperity of the adjacent continent and islands ... [depends] upon maritime activity, around such a focus of trade will centre large commercial and political interests. To protect and develop its own, each nation will seek points of support and means of influence in a quarter where the United States always has been jealously sensitive to the intrusion of European powers. The precise value of the Monroe Doctrine is understood very loosely by most Americans, but the effect of the familiar phrase has been to develop a national sensitiveness, which is a more frequent cause of war than material interests; and over disputes caused by such feelings there will preside none of the calming influence due to the moral authority of international law, with its recognized principles, for the points in dispute will be of policy, of interest, not of conceded right.

# II

## THE EUROPEAN POWERS AND VENEZUELA

Old World powers expanded their commercial activities in Central and South America throughout the latter nineteenth century. During the Venezuelan crisis of 1902, the United States began to realize how political entanglements could grow out of economic conditions. ☐ From the book *Adventures in American Diplomacy 1896-1906* by Alfred L. P. Dennis, pp. 283, 285-286, 289-292. Copyright, 1928, by E. P. Dutton & Co., Inc. Condensed by permission of the publishers.

[Let] us recall for a moment the trend of German policy during the years just prior to 1901. The growth of the . . . [German] navy was of course of particular interest to the United States. Ambassador [to Germany, Henry] White was telegraphing about the growth of the German naval budget as early as 1897 and about the establishment of a South American squadron. . . .

Germany, Great Britain, and Italy each had certain claims that they had been unable to collect from Venezuela who had treated all three of these powers with contempt. This frivolous policy on the part of Venezuela was now to meet with punishment. Germany and Great Britain had proposed in the spring of 1901 that Venezuela should submit these claims to arbitration. This President Castro refused to do. Finally in December, 1901, the German government suggested to the United States that some measures of coercion might be applied. It declared, however, that "under no circumstances do we consider in our proceedings the acquisition or the permanent occupation of Venezuelan territory." If a blockade should not be sufficient "we would have to consider the temporary occupation on our part of different Venezuelan harbor places and the levying of duties in those places." To this statement Secretary Hay replied, saying that the President believed that no measures could be taken by the German authorities contrary to these statements and quoted from the President's recent message to Congress. . . . "The Monroe Doctrine is a declaration that there must be no territorial aggrandizement by any non-American power at the expense of any American power on American soil. It is in no wise intended as hostile to any nation in the Old World. The President further said: This doctrine has nothing to do with the commercial relations of any American power, save that it in truth allows each of them to form such as it desires.... We do not guarantee any State against punishment if it misconducts itself, provided that punishment does not take the form of the acquisition of territory by any non-American power."...

...The blockade, which was the cause of much friction but which was maintained, apparently with the acquiescence of the United States, was finally lifted in the middle of February [1903]....

There remains the question of President Roosevelt's interference to persuade Germany that she should accept arbitration. For this there are only three historical documents available to me all of which are from the President's hand. Two are letters of 1906.... The extract from the private letter to Mr. [Henry] White reads as follows: "At the time of the Venezuela business I saw the German Ambassador privately myself; told him to tell the Kaiser that I had put Dewey in charge of our fleet to manoeuvre in West Indian waters; that the world at large should know this merely as a manoeuvre and we should strive in every way to appear simply as co-operating with the Germans; but that I regretted to say that the popular feeling was such that I should be obliged to interfere, by force if necessary, if the Germans took any action which looked like the acquisition of territory there or elsewhere along the Caribbean; that this was not in any way intended as a threat; but as the position on the part of the Government which the American people would demand, and that I wanted him to understand it before the two nations drifted into such a position that trouble might come....

This demonstration of the "big stick" had not taken place without careful consideration of the alternatives. A naval memorandum of the end of November, 1902, bears this out. On the possible collection of money from Venezuela by Germany this reads as follows:

"1st. There would be but little use in Germany's occupying one port only, as such action would divert trade to others. She must occupy all custom houses.

"2nd. Castro is a perfectly irresponsible dictator and would violently oppose such action. He might prohibit all local trade with the ports occupied, causing a congestion of goods there and consequent stoppage of trade, and consequently of customs receipts.

"3rd. Castro would probably oppose military resistance, and this action would bring about war with Germany. . . . While not seeking war with Venezuela, Germany once started on her expedition, would not go out of her way to avoid it.

"4th. In the event of war, Germany *must* win, to preserve her prestige. It would cost her much in men and money.

"5th. After winning she would certainly demand indemnity for her expenses.

"6th. Venezuela could not pay indemnity, and could offer nothing but territory, or mortgage her revenue in such a way as to place herself in complete political dependence on Germany.

"7th. The United States could not allow either of these, and yet Germany's right to indemnity would be incontestable.

"8th. The only courses open to the United States are the payment of the indemnity, taking such security as she can from Venezuela, or war. The first method is cheapest, the second most probable.

"9th. The United States with this possibility in view must not allow Germany during its attempt on Venezuela to occupy, fit up, or fortify any port so as to allow of its being used as a base against us. No fortifications protecting entrances of harbors, or collection of materials for such fortifications can be tolerated. . . ."

Such a memorandum would seem to indicate that in the opinion of the navy we were not prepared for war in 1902. But we were most emphatically ready.

# III

## TWO COROLLARIES TO THE MONROE DOCTRINE

The Venezuelan crisis of 1902 produced two responses, one from Luis Drago, Argentine minister of foreign affairs, the other from President Theodore Roosevelt. Excerpts from the Drago Doctrine are included in the first of the following readings. ☐ From the book *Adventures in American Diplomacy 1896-1906* by Alfred L. P. Dennis, pp. 292-293. Copyright, 1928, by E. P. Dutton & Co., Inc. Condensed by permission of the publishers.

Dr. Drago, of the Argentine Republic, put forward a doctrine, since known by his name, which asserted that force should not be used in the collection of debts. This was done in a note dated December 29, 1902. . . . In a few paragraphs it was declared that the Monroe doctrine had as its corollary the Drago doctrine. I quote in part: "At the outset it is to be noted in this connection that the capitalist who lends his money to a foreign state always takes into account the resources of the country and the probability, greater or less, that the obligations contracted will be fulfilled without delay.

"All governments thus enjoy different credit according to their degree of civilization and culture and their conduct in business transactions; and these conditions are measured and weighed before making any loan, the terms being made more or less onerous in accordance with the precise data concerning them which bankers always have on record.

"In the first place the lender knows that he is entering into a contract with a sovereign entity, and it is an inherent qualification of all sovereignty that no proceedings for the execution of a judgment may be instituted or carried out against it, since this manner of collection would compromise its very existence and cause the independence and freedom of action of the respective government to disappear.

"Among the fundamental principles of public international law which humanity has consecrated, one of the most precious is that which decrees that all states, whatever be the force at their disposal, are entitled in law, perfectly equal one to the other and mutually entitled by virtue thereof to the same consideration and respect.

"The acknowledgment of the debt, the payment of it in its entirety, can and must be made by the nation without diminution of its inherent rights as a sovereign entity, but the summary and immediate collection at a given moment, by means of force, would occasion nothing less than the ruin of the weakest nations, and the absorption of their governments . . . by the mighty of the earth. . . .

"The collection of loans by military means implies territorial occupation to make them effective, and territorial occupation signifies the suppression or subordination of the governments of the countries on which it is imposed."

This doctrine was discussed at the Third Pan-American Conference at Rio de Janiero in 1906 and . . . [was adopted by] the second Hague Conference in 1907.

The Roosevelt Corollary first appeared as part of the President's address to Congress in December 1904. ☐ Authority of Congress, *Messages and Papers of the Presidents*, Volume 15, pp. 6923-6924. New York: Bureau of National Literature, Inc.

Any country whose people conduct themselves well can count upon our hearty friendship. If a nation shows that it knows how to act with reasonable efficiency and decency in social and political matters, if it keeps order and pays its obligations, it need fear no interference from the United States. Chronic wrongdoing, or an impotence which results in a general loosening of the ties of civilized society, may in America, as elsewhere, ultimately require intervention by some civilized nation, and in the Western Hemisphere the adherence of the United States to the Monroe Doctrine may force the United States, however reluctantly, in flagrant cases of such wrongdoing or impotence, to the exercise of an international police power. . . . It is a mere truism to say that every nation, whether in America or anywhere else, which desires to maintain its freedom, its independence, must ultimately realize that the right of such independence can not be separated from the responsibility of making good use of it.

# IV

## ROOSEVELT INTERVENES IN SANTO DOMINGO

Acting on the principles which he set forth in the Roosevelt Corollary, President Theodore Roosevelt worked to keep European interests out of the Western Hemisphere. The following excerpt explains why and how the President intervened in Santo Domingo in 1905. □ Theodore Roosevelt, An Autobiography, pp. 575-579. New York: Charles Scribner's Sons, copyright 1925.

The Monroe Doctrine lays down the rule that the western hemisphere is not hereafter to be treated as subject to settlement and occupation by Old World powers. It is not international law; but it is a cardinal principle of our foreign policy. There is no difficulty at the present day in maintaining this doctrine, save where the American power whose interest is threatened has shown itself in international matters both weak and delinquent. . . .

The case was (and is) widely different as regards certain—not all—of the tropical states in the neighborhood of the Caribbean Sea. Where these states are stable and prosperous, they stand on a footing of absolute equality with all other communities. But some of them have been a prey to such continuous revolutionary misrule as to have grown impotent either to do their duties to outsiders or to enforce their rights against outsiders. . . .

. . . During the early years of my administration Santo Domingo was in its usual condition of chronic revolution. There was always fighting, always plundering; and the successful graspers for governmental power were always pawning ports and custom-houses, or trying to put them up as guaranties for loans. Of course the foreigners who made loans under such conditions demanded exorbitant interest, and if they were Europeans expected their governments to stand by them. So utter was the disorder that on one occasion when Admiral Dewey landed to pay a call of ceremony on the president, he and his party were shot at by revolutionists in crossing the square, and had to return to the ships, leaving the call unpaid. There was default on the interest due to the creditors; and finally the latter insisted upon their governments intervening. Two or three of the European powers were endeavoring to arrange for concerted action, and I was finally notified that these powers intended to take and hold several of the seaports which held custom-houses. . . .

It was the custom-houses that caused the trouble, for they offered the only means of raising money, and the revolutions were carried on to get possession of them. Accordingly I secured an agreement [early 1905] with the governmental authorities, who for the moment seemed best able to speak for the country, by which these custom-houses were placed under American control. The arrangement was that we should keep order and prevent any interference with the custom-houses or the places where they stood, and should collect the revenues. Forty-five per cent of the revenue was then turned over to the Santo Domingan Government, and fifty-five per cent put in a sinking fund in New York for the benefit of the creditors. The arrangement worked in capital style. On the forty-five per cent basis the Santo Domingan Government received from us a larger sum than it had ever received before when nominally all the revenue went to it. The creditors were . . . satisfied . . . , and no excuse for interference by European powers remained.

# V

## A LATIN AMERICAN SPEAKS

Luis Quintanilla, a twentieth-century Mexican diplomat, analyzed the justice of the Roosevelt Corollary in 1943. Although the following excerpt does not speak about the Latin American feeling as it existed in 1904, it reflects attitudes which developed gradually, as a direct result of the events at the turn of the century.   □ Luis Quintanilla, *A Latin American Speaks*, pp. 112-115, 122, 130. New York: The Macmillan Company, copyright 1943.

. . . [It] may be said that historically there are *two* Monroe Doctrines: the one, promulgated by the President; and the other, the distorted Doctrine of the Corollaries. But the authentic one has been pushed into the background. Today people have not in mind the mild offering of the fifth President of the United States, but the subsequent concoction into which entered all the imperialistic ingredients added by more voracious occupants of the White House, among whom Theodore Roosevelt—twenty-sixth President of the United States of America—stands out conspicuously. . . .

. . . Reuben Clark, most unbiased *official* United States interpreter, writes: "The United States determines *when* and *if* the principles of the Doctrine are violated, and when and if violation is threatened. We *alone* determine what measures, if any, shall be taken to vindicate the principles of the Doctrine, and *we* of necessity determine when the principles have been vindicated. No *other* power in the world has *any* relationship to, or voice in, the implementing of the principles which the Doctrine contains. It is *our* Doctrine, to be by *us* invoked and sustained, held in abeyance, or abandoned as *our* high international policy or vital national interest shall seem to *us,* and to *us alone,* to demand." Here again, I have italicized some words to bring out the point. . . .

. . . It was the expression of a wish: to remove from the Western Hemisphere the threat of European military or political interference. But there was never mention of specific measures to be taken, should that wish go unheeded. . . .

. . . Originally it meant, "America not for Europe," but the Corollaries made it say, "America for the U.S.A." Cuba, Puerto Rico, Panama, the Dominican Republic, Haiti, Nicaragua—six United States "protectorates" in less than fifteen years. . . .

. . . The days in which a single country—however powerful—could claim the exclusive right to behave, on the world stage, as a "rugged individualist," are gone forever. . . . Civilized order is a joint enterprise, freely accepted by all partners. Mankind does not allow gangsters, be they individuals or nations. Order was established, first among the members of the family, then among the residents of the community, later among the citizens of a nation. Finally the day is near when a cooperative international order will be established among the nations of the earth. That order, whether local or national, continental or international, can be conceived only as a joint enterprise. America was the first continent in history to struggle for the establishment of such order.

PROBLEM 7

The Problem of Neutrality

In 1914 war broke out in Europe. President Woodrow Wilson immediately issued a proclamation of neutrality, going on record that the United States would not take sides in the war and that it expected the belligerent powers to respect its neutral rights.

The President's act reflected American wishes to keep out of the war. In 1914 the United States had no clear policy toward Europe other than its traditional position of non-involvement in overseas affairs. In addition, loyalties and sympathies were divided. Millions of Americans, those born in Europe and the first-generation Americans born of immigrant parents, had sympathies for the belligerents. American neutrality was also influenced by a strong humanitarian opposition to war as a means of settling differences. The United States hoped that, as a neutral, it could help bring about a "just peace," a peace to prevent postwar hatreds and possible later wars of revenge.

Whenever war occurs in the world the foreign policy makers of any nation must consider not only immediate goals and interests but also probable long-term results. They must weigh the hard realities of conflict as well as humanitarian ideals. With these considerations in mind, neutrality seemed to be the wisest course for the United States to follow at the time. Yet, whether neutrality would continue to serve American interests would depend upon the course of events in Europe.

Wilson insisted that Britain and Germany respect the American right to trade with belligerents or with other neutrals, regardless of the final destination of the goods. Both powers violated American freedom of the seas; since industrial, financial, and agricultural interests depended upon foreign trade for prosperity, this interference affected the American economy. It became evident that the neutral rights established upon ideal principles of justice during peacetime could not be maintained in wartime.

Nevertheless, the American public and national leaders hoped to avoid involvement. In the summer and fall of 1916 the slogan "He kept us out of war" played a great part in Wilson's campaign for re-election. But in early 1917, unrestricted submarine warfare by Germany forced the United States to abandon neutrality. On April 2, 1917, the President called Congress into special session and asked for a declaration of war against Germany. "The world," he said, "must be made safe for democracy." As you read, consider the following questions:

1    How did both Britain and Germany attempt to restrict United States commerical activities between 1914 and 1917?

2    Why did the United States increasingly favor Britain and blame Germany in the war?

3    Why did Lippmann think that the United States abandoned neutrality? Why did Barnes think that the United States abandoned neutrality? Which author, in your opinion, had better reasons?

4    How did national interests and the international situation change between 1914 and 1917? Was the United States justified in declaring war on Germany? Why?

5    Do you agree with this statement? "The circumstances of the war indicate clearly that a nation can determine its foreign policy as it wishes, and can remain neutral if it wants to be." Why?

# I

## BELLIGERENT ACTIONS THREATEN NEUTRALITY

Both Britain and Germany threatened to destroy neutral shipping between 1914 and 1917. Because each one interfered with American rights on the seas,

either belligerent could have provoked the United States to war. Charles Seymour, historian and educator, described the British blockade of neutral goods into Germany. The following reading, containing Seymour's description, thus explains why the United States might have gone to war with Britain.
☐ Charles Seymour, *American Diplomacy During the World War,* pp. 27-28, 31, 35. Baltimore: The Johns Hopkins Press, copyright 1934.

[The] Allies were bound to capitalize [their command of the seas] to the full. In a short war it might turn the scale; if the struggle were prolonged it would be deadly. Germany was dependent upon imports both for the physical means of conducting war and for the equally vital maintenance of national morale. The problem of raw materials and foodstuffs hung its shadow over her from beginning to end. It was the business of the Allies to cut off those imports to the last ton.

The process led inevitably to conflict with the interests and the feelings of neutrals, especially of the greatest of neutrals, the United States. The belligerent in command of the seas naturally claims the utmost extension of restrictions upon the Freedom of the Seas compatible with existing circumstances. He is restrained to some extent by the recognition of neutral rights, as expressed in custom or special conventions—so-called international law. He is restrained much more forcibly by the necessity of conciliating the neutrals, for sea power is determined less by rules than by circumstances. . . . The commanding sea power, be it the Northern States in the Civil War or the British in the World War, would not permit an ill-defined "international law" to interfere with measures apparently essential to national existence. Mr. [Herbert H.] Asquith [British Prime Minister] made practical confession of such determination. "We are not going to allow our efforts," he told the House of Commons on March 1, 1915, "to be strangled in a network of juridical niceties. . . . Under existing conditions there is no form of economic pressure to which we do not consider ourselves entitled to resort." . . .

. . . [The British] felt compelled . . . to substitute for an official blockade a series of processes that would have the same economic effects on Germany, by an interruption of the trade of neutral ports which might serve Germany as a base of supplies. Roughly speaking, those processes were of three kinds. In the first place the Allies extended the traditional principle of the belligerent's right to seize contraband, by adding to the list of contraband articles, by finding justification for the seizure of conditional contraband, and by the control of neutral vessels through the right of visit and search. In the second place, contending that German infractions of maritime law gave the Allies the right to reprisals, they proceeded to interrupt all commerce whatsoever with Germany . . . . Finally they introduced a third general policy, that of rationing the neutrals of northern Europe, permitting them to import only sufficient for their normal needs and thus preventing trans-shipment to Germany. . . .

Such invasions of neutral rights, at least as understood by the United States, became more vexatious because of the mechanism of control exercised by the British navy. Allied methods quite as much as, or more than, policy infuriated American shippers, who suspected and openly alleged British plans to kill American trade under the excuse of national self-protection. They objected particularly to the development of the belligerent right of visit and search, which the Allied navies interpreted to mean the right to bring ships into port on suspicion.

The following selection is an excerpt from Secretary of State William Jennings Bryan's note of May 13, 1915, to the Imperial German Government protesting the sinking of the British ocean liner *Lusitania*. □ *Papers Relating to Foreign Affairs of the United States,* 1915 Supplement, pp. 393-396. Washington, D.C.: United States Government Printing Office.

In view of recent acts of the German authorities in violation of American rights on the high seas which culminated in the torpedoing and sinking of the British steamship *Lusitania* on May 7, 1915, by which over 100 American citizens lost their lives, it is clearly wise and desirable that the Government of the United States and the Imperial German Government should come to a clear and full understanding as to the grave situation which has resulted.

The sinking of the British passenger steamer *Falaba* by a German submarine on March 28, through which Leon C. Thrasher, an American citizen was drowned; the attack on April 28 on the American vessel *Cushing* by a German aeroplane; the torpedoing on May 1 of the American vessel *Gulflight* by a German submarine, as a result of which two or more American citizens met their death; and, finally, the torpedoing and sinking of the steamship *Lusitania,* constitute a series of events which the Government of the United States has observed with growing concern, distress, and amazement. . . .

. . . It assumes . . . that the Imperial Government accept, as of course, the rule that the lives of non-combatants, whether they be of neutral citizenship or citizens of one of the nations at war, can not lawfully or rightfully be put in jeopardy by the capture or destruction of an unarmed merchantman, and recognize also, as all other nations do, the obligation to take the usual precaution of visit and search to ascertain whether a suspected merchantman is in fact of belligerent nationality or is in fact carrying contraband of war under a neutral flag. . . .

American citizens act within their indisputable rights in taking their ships and in traveling wherever their legitimate business calls them upon the high seas, and exercise those rights in what should be the well-justified confidence that their lives will not be endangered by acts done in clear violation of universally acknowledged international obligations, and certainly in the confidence that their own Government will sustain them in the exercise of their rights. . . .

The Imperial German Government will not expect the Government of the United States to omit any word or any act necessary to the performance of its sacred duty of maintaining the rights of the United States and its citizens and of safeguarding their free exercise and enjoyment.

# II

## UNITED STATES INTERESTS AND THE WAR

Problems in maintaining neutrality were created by some Americans who profited from trade with the Allies and by others who feared for national security. In August 1915 Secretary of the Treasury William G. McAdoo supported a loan program to stimulate foreign trade. Later the same month, the administration approved such a program. ☐ "McAdoo to President Wilson, August 21, 1915." William Appleman Williams, *The Shaping of American Diplomacy*, Volume 2, pp. 584-585. Chicago: Rand McNally and Company, copyright © 1956.

You know how loath I am always to burden you with Treasury affairs, but matters of such great importance have arisen in connection with the financing of our export trade that you ought to know the facts.

Great Britain is, and always has been, our best customer. Since the war began, her purchases and those of her Allies (France, Russia, and Italy) have enormously increased. Food products constitute the greater part of these purchases, but war munitions, which as you know embrace not only arms and ammunition, but saddles, horses, and mules and a variety of things, are a big item. The high prices for food products have brought great prosperity to our farmers, while the purchases of war munitions have stimulated industry and have set factories going to full capacity throughout the great manufacturing districts, while the reduction of imports and their actual cessation in some cases, have caused new industries to spring up and others to be enlarged. Great prosperity is coming. It is, in large measure, here already. It will be tremendously increased if we can extend reasonable credits to our customers.... Our prosperity is dependent on our continued and enlarged foreign trade. To preserve that we must do everything we can to assist our customers to buy....

It is imperative for England to establish a large credit in this country. She will need at least $500,000,000. She can't get this in any way, at the moment, that seems feasible, except for sale of short-time Government notes. Here she encounters the obstacle presented by Mr. Bryan's letter of June 20, 1915, to Senator Stone in which it is stated that "war loans in this country were disapproved because inconsistent with the spirit of neutrality" etc., and "this Government has not been advised that any general loans have been made by foreign governments in this country since *the President expressed his wish that loans of this character should not be made.* The underscored part is the hardest hurdle of the entire letter. Large banking houses here which have the ability to finance a large loan, will not do so or even attempt to do so, in the face of this declaration. We have tied our hands so that we cannot help ourselves or help our best customers. France and Russia are in the same boat. Each, especially France, needs a large credit here.

The declaration seems to me most illogical and inconsistent. We approve and encourage sales of supplies to England and others but we disapprove the creation by them of credit balances here to finance their lawful and welcome purchases. We must find some way to give them needed credits but there is no way, I fear, unless this declaration can be modified. Maybe the *Arabic* incident may clarify the situation! I should hate to have it modified that way.

In late January 1917, shortly before resumption of unrestricted submarine warfare, Secretary of State Robert Lansing considered the possibility of declaring war for national security. ☐ Robert Lansing, *War Memoirs*, pp. 208-209. Indianapolis: Bobbs-Merrill Company, copyright 1935.

[To] plunge this nation into this terrible struggle is a responsibility from which a conscientious leader may well shrink, and I can understand the natural resistance of the President to the forces which are resistlessly urging him on....

Sooner or later the die will be cast and we will be at war with Germany. It is certain to come. We must nevertheless wait patiently until the Germans do something which will arouse general indignation and make all Americans alive to the peril of German success in this war. When that time comes, . . . I am convinced that the President will act and act with vigor. . . .

Looking at the situation without bias and without undue weight to our selfish interests, we can no more avoid entering this war against Germany than we can avoid the progress of time. . . .

I hate the horrors of war but I hate worse the horrors of German mastery. War cannot come too soon to suit me since I know that it must come at last.

# III

## WHY DID THE UNITED STATES GO TO WAR?

Historians have disagreed on why the United States entered World War I. The author of the following selection asserted that financial interests supported the Allied cause. □ Reprinted with deletions from *The Genesis of the World War* by Harry Elmer Barnes, copyright 1926 by Alfred A. Knopf, Inc., and renewed 1954 by Harry Elmer Barnes. Reprinted by permission of the publisher.

The alleged reason why the United States entered the War was, of course, the resumption of unlimited German submarine warfare, but to have any understanding of the deeper causes we must get at the causes for the German submarine warfare in general, as well as its resumption in January, 1917. Here we are on firm ground. There is no doubt that the German submarine warfare was developed as a counter movement against the English violation of international law in regard to blockade, contraband and continuous voyage. By practically destroying, in these respects, the rights of neutrals, which had been worked out in a century of the development of international law, Great Britain was virtually able to shut off all imports into Germany from foreign countries, not only directly but also through neutral ports. It was to retaliate against this that Germany initiated her submarine warfare, which certainly cannot be regarded as in any sense more atrocious in fact or law than those English violations of neutral rights which had produced the submarine campaign. By practically acquiescing in these British violations of international law we not only lost most of what we had gained in the past

in the way of establishing neutral rights on the seas, but also set a prec-
edent which will prove an extremely nasty and embarrassing stumbling-
block in the course of future negotiations in the event of war.

In addition to these English violations of international law which
vitally affected Germany as well as neutrals, there were many other
examples of British lawlessness, such as the interception of our mails,
the use of the American flag on British ships, the seizure and search of
United States officials below the rank of minister while traveling to and
from their continental posts, and the capture of ships ... which had
been legally transferred from enemy countries to American owners. If
the United States had held England strictly to international law upon
the threat of severance of diplomatic relations or even war, as we did in
the case of Germany and as we unquestionably should have done in the
case of England, the German submarine warfare would not have been
necessary and probably would not have been utilized. So we may say
with absolute certainty that it was the unneutrality, lack of courage, or
maladroitness of the Washington authorities in regard to English violations of international law which produced the German submarine warfare that actually led us into war. . . .

Next we should note the powerful pressure of the great American
financial interests and their subsidized press. From the beginning the
international banking houses of the United States had taken a distinctly
unneutral attitude, favoring investment in the bonds of the Allied countries, and discouraging or refusing investment in the paper of the Central
Powers. This immediately gave us a strong financial stake in the cause
of the Entente, and this stake grew larger with each year of the war.
Likewise, American industry inevitably became violently pro-Ally.
This was due to the fact that the British illegal blockade unlawfully cut
off our sales of war materials to the Central Powers and made our enormous war profits dependent upon the purchases made by Great Britain,
France, Russia and Italy. Upon the prospects of their success in the
War and their ability to prolong the conflict depended the relative
amount of American profits and the probability of our receiving payment
for the goods we sold to these Entente powers. . . .

Some have held that a powerful factor affecting Mr. Wilson's decision was his conviction by 1916 that he could not lead world policy
through pacific methods but might assume world leadership if he threw
the United States into the War and was thereby able to dominate the war
aims of the Allied powers and the United States. Many of the facts in
his conduct in the spring of 1916 and thereafter lend much plausibility to

this hypothesis. The writer believes, however, that it was his pro-British sympathy more than anything else which led Mr. Wilson into his decision by the close of 1915 that we must enter the World War unless the English objectives could be realized through a negotiated peace.

The occasion for going to war was Germany's unrestricted use of the submarine against American merchant shipping on the Atlantic routes from North America to the British Isles and France. But the substantial and compelling reason for going to war was that the cutting of the Atlantic communications meant the starvation of Britain and, therefore, the conquest of Western Europe by Imperial Germany.

President Wilson avoided this explanation of his decision to intervene, choosing instead to base his decision upon the specific legal objection to unrestricted submarine warfare and upon a generalized moral objection to lawless and cruel aggression. But these superficial reasons for the declaration of war would never have carried the day if a majority of the people had not recognized intuitively, and if some Americans had not seen clearly, what the threatened German victory would mean to the United States. Though there was lacking the tradition of a foreign policy which made the matter self-evident, many Americans saw in 1917 that if Germany won, the United States would have to face a new and aggressively expanding German empire which had made Britain, France, and Russia its vassals, and Japan its ally.... It was in this very concrete and practical sense ... that a German victory in 1917 would have made the world unsafe for the American democracies from Canada to the Argentine. . . .

Nor did the United States go to war to make the world safe for all democracies: if it had seemed probable that Germany would be defeated by Czarist Russia, the United States would have remained neutral because its vital interests in the North Atlantic would have remained secure. . . .

The United States did not go to war because it wished to found a League of Nations; it went to war in order to preserve American security. And when the war was over, the nation would almost certainly have accepted in some form or other the scheme of the League of Nations if

President Wilson had been able to demonstrate to the people that the League would perpetuate the security which the military victory had won for them. Mr. Wilson failed to make this demonstration. He failed because in leading the nation to war he had failed to give the durable and compelling reasons for the momentous decision. The reasons he did give were legalistic and moralistic and idealistic reasons, rather than the substantial and vital reason that the security of the United States demanded that no aggressively expanding imperial power, like Germany, should be allowed to gain the mastery of the Atlantic Ocean.

PROBLEM 8

Creating a Just Peace

President Woodrow Wilson's hopes for bringing the European war to a negotiated end were frustrated when, in April 1917, the United States declared war against Germany. Yet throughout the war, Wilson never lost sight of the goal of a "just peace." In his endeavor, he pursued a policy of "war on the German government, peace with the German people." And in an address to Congress in January 1918, he offered his "Fourteen Points" as the "program of the world's peace ... the only possible program." Assuming leadership of the peace movement before the war was over, Wilson appealed to the Allies and the German people for their cooperation in formulating a treaty based on the Fourteen Points. The Germans, on the brink of defeat by the autumn of 1918, were willing to negotiate a peace on the basis of Wilson's program. The Allies, however, wanted vengeance, and in preliminary armistice negotiations they did not accept all the points.

After those preliminary talks, the Allied and associated powers met from January to June 1919 at the Palace of Versailles outside Paris. The defeated nations did not participate in the framing of the peace; they were invited to Versailles only to sign the treaty.

What was also significant for the future of the treaty was that Wilson had not invited representatives of the Republican party or the Senate to participate with him in the treaty talks. In July 1919, however, he asked the Senate, which had a Republican majority, to ratify the treaty and, with it, the League of Nations.

In the American political system, treaties with foreign nations are not easy to put into effect. The United States Constitution provides that the President "shall have power, by and with the Advice and Consent of the Senate, to make Treaties, provided two thirds of the Senators present concur." In the United States, power to establish treaties is thus shared among the branches of the government. The system of checks and balances is intended to ensure that such international agreements represent the feelings of a majority of the citizens. Because the Senate is responsible for checking the President's treaty-making power, personalities, political parties, and public opinion—important aspects of the representative nature of the Senate—play vital roles in effecting foreign policy.

Opposition in the Senate to the Covenant of the League of Nations, led by Republican Henry Cabot Lodge of Massachusetts, was directed in particular at Article X, which stated that members would "undertake to respect and preserve as against external aggression the territorial integrity and existing political independence of all Members of the League" and that "the Council shall advise upon the means." Many Americans believed with Lodge that through the treaty the United States would be committed to an "entangling alliance" and that other nations could determine its foreign policy by obliging it to participate in action against aggressors.

Deciding that an appeal to the country would force the Senate into line for the necessary two-thirds vote, President Wilson traveled over 8,000 miles by train and spoke forty times in twenty-two days. He became ill, and was forced to abandon his appeal. Wilson never succeeded in mustering enough votes to have the treaty passed as he had originally proposed it. Yet his belief in the original proposal was so intense that he used his influence to keep his supporters from agreeing to the changes which could have brought passage.

As you read, consider the following questions:

1    In assuming leadership of the peace movement after World War I, what attitudes did Wilson show toward American political parties and American public opinion? Was he carrying out his proper role as President in taking such action?

**2**    What strategy did Lodge use to defeat the League of Nations, some form of which the majority of Americans were presumably willing to accept? In opposing Wilson, was Lodge properly carrying out his role as a legislative leader? Were his tactics legitimate? Do you think that they were wise?

**3**    What do you think were the fundamental and vital issues at stake in the controversy between Lodge and Wilson over the League?

**4**    Do you think that the American democratic form of government was adequate to deal vigorously with the complexities of the peace negotiations following World War I?

# I

## LODGE AND THE DEFEAT OF THE TREATY

Personalities played a significant part in defeating the Treaty of Versailles in the Senate. Alexander and Juliette George explained how Senator Lodge encouraged the defeat of the treaty as Wilson had proposed it.    ☐ Reprinted by permission of the authors from Alexander L. George and Juliette L. George, *Woodrow Wilson and Colonel House*, pp. 268-271, 273-274, 276-278. The John Day Company, Inc., 1956. Paperback edition, Dover Publications, Inc., 1964.

All the time President Wilson was in Paris spending himself to the utmost first to secure the League Covenant and then to amend it, his enemies at home, led by Senator Lodge, plotted his defeat. . . .

Lodge, indeed, did not even have to examine the Covenant to be certain that it was a dangerous proposition. He had long since decided that while it would be "a mistake" to reject the *idea* of a league of nations — everyone, after all, favored the preservation of world peace — it would be possible to confound any practical plan, no matter what its terms. . . .

Throughout the battle over Senate ratification of the Treaty of Versailles, Lodge piously maintained that his position was dictated by an overriding concern for safeguarding the interests of the United States, and that he favored American entry into the League of Nations if only the Covenant could be so changed that basic American interests would be protected. It was widely suspected at the time, and frequently has been suggested since, that Lodge was out first and foremost to humiliate President Wilson, and that he had no use whatever for Wilson's League in any form. Since a policy of outright rejection would surely fail because of widespread public endorsement of the League, Lodge shrewdly feigned a more moderate position. He did so, according to this theory, the better ultimately to kill Wilson's creation or, at the very least, to change it and force the proud President to bow to the Republican-controlled Senate, thus yielding prestige, both personal and political.

In the light of Lodge's maneuvers throughout the Treaty fight, this interpretation is persuasive. It gains all but irresistible plausibility from the fact that when at last the Senate rejected the Treaty, League and all, Lodge felt, as he declared in a letter, that he and his colleagues had done very well. To one of his Senate colleagues, he referred to the outcome of the controversy as a "victory." Further, at the Republican Convention of 1920, Lodge refused to urge ratification of the Treaty with the reservations he had so vociferously advocated but preferred, instead, to leave the way open for a complete repudiation of the League. And when, indeed, the Republicans won the election of 1920, Lodge exultantly declared that so far as the United States was concerned, the League of Nations was dead.

Lodge personally detested Wilson, a fact to which his letters and papers eloquently testify. Quite apart from this highly personal consideration, however, as a Republican political leader Lodge had his eye upon the next presidential election, an event which has seldom failed to magnify the partisan component of issues before Congress for long months before its occurrence. . . .

Wilson had deep-seated doubts, which originated in his early years, of his intellectual competence, his moral worth and his strength. He had tried to overcome these self-doubts by rigorous training and ceaseless self-vindicating demonstrations through accomplishment that he was indeed of superior intelligence, of good and "unselfish" character, and of sufficient strength to escape the degradation of capitulating to anybody. With an unerring sense of where his adversary's weak points lay and with an air of patronizing superiority, Lodge peppered him with just those personal attacks which intensified Wilson's inner anxieties. . . .

President Wilson arrived home from Europe on July 8, 1919. Two days later he appeared before the Senate to lay the Treaty before it for ratification. Shortly before leaving the White House to address the Senate, Wilson held a press conference. One of the reporters inquired whether the Treaty would pass if the Senate attached reservations to it. "I do not think hypothetical questions are concerned," Wilson flashed back. *"The Senate is going to ratify the treaty."*

If his address to the Senate had a somewhat less peremptory tone, its plain implication was the same: the Senate *must* ratify the Treaty — it was God's will. It was not a perfect instrument, the President conceded. Many "minor compromises" had been made but, he declared euphemistically, the settlement "squares, as a whole, with the principles agreed upon as the basis of the peace...." The Treaty's most important accomplishment was the creation of the League of Nations. "Dare we reject it and break the heart of the world?" Rejection was unthinkable. America, as had been universally recognized, "entered the war to promote no private or peculiar interest of her own but only as the champion of rights which she was glad to share with free men and lovers of justice everywhere." Now the world looked to America for moral leadership, and it was our duty to accept the responsibility of providing it....

The Treaty having been formally placed before the Senate, it was immediately referred to the Senate Foreign Relations Committee. The chairman of this Committee, of course, was Henry Cabot Lodge.

Though chairman of the Foreign Relations Committee and leader of the majority party in the Senate ... Lodge was in an extremely difficult position. The nub of his dilemma was that public opinion overwhelmingly favored *a* league, and, after Wilson succeeded in amending the Covenant in Paris to eliminate most of the dangers its opponents professed to see in it, the public plainly favored *the* League. Several polls testified to that fact. So did the tidal wave of favorable comment in the press and in lecture halls and pulpits throughout the land, of resolutions of endorsement by farm and labor organizations and by state legislatures.

Senator Lodge was greatly concerned over this state of affairs. He was shrewd enough to realize that, given the temper of the country and even of a goodly number of his Republican colleagues in the Senate, any immediate showdown between the supporters of the League and its opponents would result in a rout of the latter....

Lodge accordingly felt that it was necessary to gain time to influence opinion against the Treaty as it stood....

From a strictly partisan point of view, it would never do to allow Wilson, singlehanded, the great accomplishment of which he dreamed. On the heels of such a success, the Republicans feared, he might seek a third term — and might even win it. From the Republican point of view, Wilson's League must either be defeated or, at the very least, so "Republicanized" that the GOP could claim credit for some of its good features. That the Treaty would be ratified and the United States would enter the League, however, seemed a foregone conclusion. A large proportion of Republican Senators were willing to content themselves with making only minor changes in the Treaty. They, together with the Democrats, constituted a majority of the Senate and could probably attract sufficient additional votes to make up the necessary two-thirds for ratification. . . .

Lodge's whole plan of action was based upon his estimate that Wilson would never consent to accepting Senate reservations to the Treaty. To Lodge . . . Wilson "was simply an element to be calmly and cooly considered in a great problem of international politics." It was the Senator's "calm" and "cool" judgment that Wilson would do all he could to "prevent the acceptance of the treaty with reservations. . . ."

Given this conviction and the intrepidity to stake his whole strategy on it, Lodge was able to map out a plan of action at once beautifully simple and subtle. All he had to do was tack reservations onto the Treaty, and most particularly onto the League Covenant, which Wilson held so dear. Then, if his theory was correct, Wilson could be counted on himself to destroy what he had invested his lifeblood to create.

# II

## WILSON AND THE DEFEAT OF THE TREATY

Arthur S. Link, well-known for his work as biographer of Wilson and editor of the Wilson papers, tried to explain the President's actions as reflections of his character. The following excerpt is concerned with Wilson's reasons for encouraging defeat of the League. □ Arthur S. Link, *Wilson the Diplomatist*, pp. 153-155. Baltimore: The Johns Hopkins Press, copyright © 1957.

Virtually all historians now agree that Wilson's refusal to permit his followers in the Senate to approve the treaty with the Lodge reservations was an error of tragic magnitude. Having built so grandly at Paris, having fought so magnificently at home for his creation, he then proceeded by his own hand to remove the cornerstone of his edifice of peace. Why? Were there inner demons of pride and arrogance driving him to what one historian had called "the supreme infanticide"? Did his illness and seclusion [following physical collapse in September 1919] prevent him from obtaining a realistic view of the parliamentary situation, or so disarrange him emotionally that he became incompetent in the tasks of statesmanship? Or was he simply an idealist who would make no compromises on what he thought were fundamental principles?

...Wilson, for all his highmindedness and nobility of character, was headstrong and not much given to dealing graciously or to compromising with men whom he distrusted and disliked. ... The sympathetic biographer would like to believe that it was his illness, which aggravated his bitterness and his sense of self-righteousness, that drove Wilson to his fatal choice. Perhaps this is true. He had not always been incapable of compromise; perhaps he would have yielded in the end if disease had not dethroned his reason.

These attempts to extenuate ignore the fact that there were fundamental and vital issues at stake in the controversy over the treaty— whether the United States would take leadership in the League of Nations without hesitations and reservations, or whether it would join the League grudgingly and with no promises to help maintain universal collective security. To Wilson the difference between what he fought for and what Lodge and the Republicans would agree to was the difference between the success or failure and the life or death of man's best hope for peace. This he had said on his western tour, at a time when his health and reasoning faculties were unimpaired. This he believed with his heart and soul. It is, therefore, possible, even probable, that Wilson would have acted as he did even had he not suffered his breakdown, for it was not in his nature to compromise away the principles in which he believed.

If this is true, then in this, the last and greatest effort of his life, Wilson spurned the role of statesman for what he must have thought was the nobler role of prophet. The truth is that the American people were not prepared in 1920 to assume the world leadership that Wilson offered them, and that the powers of the world were not yet ready to enforce the world-wide, universal system of collective security that the President created.

# III

## POLITICAL INTERESTS vs. HUMANITARIAN CONSIDERATIONS

Political parties were important to the fate of the treaty in the Senate. Political scientist Denna Frank Fleming criticized the narrow partisanship exercised by the Republicans during the Senate debate on the Treaty of Versailles.  □ Denna Frank Fleming, *The United States and World Organization 1920-1933*, pp. 20-22, 31-32. New York: Columbia University Press, copyright 1938.

[To] weaken the President before he arrived in Paris, Senator [Philander C.] Knox [Republican from Pennsylvania] introduced a resolution in the Senate, on December 3 [1918], declaring that any project for a league of nations should be postponed for consideration, "if and when at some future time general conferences on those subjects might be deemed useful."

It is doubtful if a more brazen, presumptuous demand has ever been made by a group of politicians in any country. After the life of the whole world had been disrupted by a breakdown of international order that was stupid and inexcusable, even if it was not criminally planned as was then generally believed, the . . . Senate leaders [Republicans] could think of nothing better to do than to forbid any immediate effort to organize against a similar calamity. After they had read during long years of the death or mutilation, of the physical and mental agony of hundreds of millions of their own race, they could be guilty of thinking only of schemes to defeat the President of their own nation to whom the stricken multitudes of every land looked for assurance against a return of the scourge. While devoted men everywhere strained to catch the opportunity to build some foundations for a safer world, before the nations should be turned away from any high endeavor by their renewed dissensions, disorganization, and daily cares, the Senators could only urge that any effort to advance be halted until a Republican President had been elected. . . .

. . . What they demanded was nothing less than that the whole of outraged humanity should make no advance upon the path of international organization, upon which it had already proceeded far before the war, until they should give the word and assume the leadership. The historian may search long before he comes upon an equal example of upstart effrontery. . . .

. . . Lodge, too, was totally unmoved by the worldwide sweep of the war. He actually protested against "trying to provide against wars which may never be fought" and warned that if any "extraneous provision" were "unwisely added" to the treaty, such provisions "would surely be stricken out or amended, no matter how many signatures might be added to a treaty. Protracted opposition and amendments mean long delays, and delay is only less fortunate than rejection."

This warning was plainly and admittedly directed at the leaders of the Allied Powers in the hope that they would ignore Wilson. The leaders of the United States Senate, by grace of a majority of two, served notice upon the congress of nations then gathering that no advance in international organization would be permitted at that time, "no matter how many" nations desired it. Whatever was attempted would be obstructed as long as might be necessary. . . .

. . . [The] Treaty with the Lodge reservations attached failed of approval finally on March 19, 1920, . . . by a vote of 49 to 35, seven votes short of the required two-thirds majority. . . .

. . . Republican voters were sure to censure Wilson for failing to permit their ruling leaders to make at least a few little changes in the Covenant. The strategy adopted by Lodge and his associates in the beginning was fundamentally sound. Never-ending questioning can remodel or defeat any treaty that may be negotiated hereafter, so long as two-thirds vote for treaties is required in the Senate.

# IV

### WHO KILLED THE TREATY?

Thomas A. Bailey centered his attention on domestic issues which influenced the fight over the League of Nations. The following excerpt reviews the conflict between Lodge and Wilson and then asks who was responsible for the failure of the treaty in the Senate. ☐ Reprinted with permission of The Macmillan Company from *Woodrow Wilson and the Great Betrayal* by Thomas A. Bailey, pp. 85-86, 154, 157, 167, 271, 277. Copyright 1945 by Thomas A. Bailey.

This was the first that a President had ever consented to meet the Foreign Relations Committee at the White House and be publicly grilled by it. . . .

Much of the discussion centered about Article X, which had been pictured by its foes as an agency to beget war rather than to promote peace. Wilson made it clear that he not only regarded Article X as the "backbone" of the covenant, but that he as much as anyone was the author of it. He pointed out that since the Article was permissive in its obligations, it was morally rather than legally binding. No superbody could order us about, he said, for *in any given case we would consult our consciences and act accordingly.* . . .

. . . Lodge presented from the Committee on Foreign Relations, on November 6, 1919, a series of fourteen reservations. . . .

The Lodge reservation to Article X declared that the United States "assumes no obligation" to preserve the independence or territorial integrity of any other country, or to employ the armed forces of the United States for such purpose, *unless* Congress should so provide.

We must note at the outset that the Lodge reservation did not wipe out Article X. This article could still function. The basic general obligation in the first sentence was left untouched. We *might* be willing to cooperate with other nations in employing our army and navy. But first Congress, which ... possesses the war-declaring power, would have to vote its approval. . . . But Wilson was unalterably opposed to the Lodge reservation because it specifically removed any *moral* obligation to exercise that free choice against the aggressor. It was, in his mind, a "knife thrust at the heart of the treaty."

It is difficult at this distance to understand why Wilson should have been determined to block all compromise, and with it the treaty, over the Lodge reservation to Article X. Actually, the more important articles which provided the machinery and the teeth of the League were left untouched or virtually untouched.

. . . If the people of the United States were unwilling to support it, the absence of reservations probably would have availed little; if the American people were willing to support it, the Lodge reservations did not prevent them from doing so. . . .

[When the treaty failed to achieve a two-thirds vote in the Senate, who had killed it?]

The vital role of the loyal Democrats must be reemphasized. If all of them who professed to want the treaty had voted "Yea," it would have passed with more than a dozen votes to spare. If the strait-jacket of party loyalty had not been involved, the necessary two-thirds could easily have been mustered. . . .

Wilson had said that the reservation to Article X was a knife thrust at the heart of the Covenant. Ironically, he parried this knife thrust, and stuck his own dagger, not into the heart of the Covenant, but into the entire treaty.

This was the supreme paradox. He who had forced the Allies to write the League into the treaty, unwrote it; he who had done more than any other man to make the Covenant, unmade it—at least so far as America was concerned. And by his action, he contributed powerfully to the ultimate undoing of the League, and with it the high hopes of himself and mankind for an organization to prevent World War II.

PROBLEM 9

# Republicans, Pacifism, and Policy

World War I was ended. In its promise to lead Americans back to "normalcy," the Republican party declared in 1920 that the United States should stand for "agreement among nations to preserve the peace of the world." It also asserted that the United States should support the "time-honored policies in favor of peace declared by Washington, Jefferson, and Monroe." The importance of this vague statement of policy was that it brought together the internationalists, who sought peace through cooperative action, and the isolationists, who strove to avoid involvement in European affairs. Partly because it accommodated both extremes in its statement of policy, the Republican party won a smashing victory in 1920 and remained in power until 1933.

Interpreting the Republican victory in 1920 as a mandate against the League of Nations, the new administration was faced with the problem of establishing a different policy which would satisfy both the isolationists and the internationalists. At first the United States was so anxious to ignore the League that American officials refused to open mail from that body. The absurdity of the situation finally forced the United States into cooperation with several League conferences on specific world problems. Despite this limited cooperation in League programs, the United States did not join the Permanent Court of International Justice, the League tribunal commonly known as the World Court. Although an American had served as a justice from the beginning, the United States would not submit to the judgments of the Court.

In the attempt to establish a constructive foreign policy during the 1920's, the United States declared a dedication to peace. But at the same time, it assumed a dedication to national security, which implied defensive preparedness for war. Attempting to gain these goals, the United States cooperated with other nations by entering into multilateral pacts to limit armaments, to limit territorial expansion, and to outlaw war. In 1921 the United States called a conference of nine powers who had interests in the Pacific to set a limitation on naval armaments. This Washington Naval Conference was successful in establishing that limitation and was hailed at the time as a great step toward peace. In the Four Power and Nine Power Treaties of 1921 and 1922, the signatories tried to prevent war by agreeing to respect the territorial *status quo* in the Pacific.

In another attempt to use the spirit of internationalism creatively without violating the strong American fear of military or legal commitments to other nations, the United States helped frame the Kellogg-Briand Treaty, sometimes known as the Pact of Paris, in 1928. George W. Wickersham, commenting on the treaty in the April 1929 issue of *Foreign Affairs,* said: "The fact, that immediately following the vote, the Senate proceeded to the consideration of a bill authorizing the construction of fifteen cruisers, to which a large number of Senators obviously were committed, accentuated their lack of conviction in the reality of the peace treaty, and a willingness that that august body should appear like the temple of Janus, with two heads—one contemplating peace and the other smiling at war!"

As you read, consider the following questions:

1    How did the Kellogg-Briand Treaty attempt to solve the problem of satisfying both the isolationists and the internationalists?

2    Why do you think that the members of the Senate passed the treaty as it stood despite the fact that many felt it would not prevent war?

3    Do you think that the Kellogg-Briand Treaty was a good solution to the international problems of the 1920's? Was it possible for the Republicans to develop a strong foreign policy at that time? Why?

4    How do you think that the treaty might have been changed or interpreted to stop the Japanese aggression in 1931?

**5**    How do you think the Kellogg-Briand Treaty affected the League of Nations?

# I

## THE KELLOGG-BRIAND TREATY

After the war, France sought to guarantee its safety from the possibility of another German attack with bilateral military alliances. In the spring of 1927, French Foreign Minister Aristide Briand proposed his Pact of Perpetual Friendship to the United States. But the United States, sensing Briand's primary concern for French security, did not want to commit itself to possible involvement in a future European war. Secretary of State Frank B. Kellogg, under intense pressure from the well-organized and vocal American peace movement, made a counter-proposal to Briand for a multilateral treaty for the renunciation of war. In this way, Kellogg successfully side stepped a definite commitment to France. Briand did not want a multilateral treaty, but he could not easily refuse to sign an agreement renouncing war. The following reading is excerpted from the treaty signed at Paris on August 27, 1928.   □ *United States Statutes at Large*, Volume 46, pp. 2343-2347.

THE PRESIDENT OF THE GERMAN REICH, THE PRESIDENT OF THE UNITED STATES OF AMERICA, HIS MAJESTY THE KING OF THE BELGIANS, THE PRESIDENT OF THE FRENCH REPUBLIC, HIS MAJESTY THE KING OF GREAT BRITAIN, IRELAND AND THE BRITISH DOMINIONS BEYOND THE SEAS, EMPEROR OF INDIA, HIS MAJESTY THE KING OF ITALY, HIS MAJESTY THE EMPEROR OF JAPAN, THE PRESIDENT OF THE REPUBLIC OF POLAND, THE PRESIDENT OF THE CZECHOSLOVAK REPUBLIC,

Deeply sensible of their solemn duty to promote the welfare of mankind;

Persuaded that the time has come when a frank renunciation of war as an instrument of national policy should be made to the end that the peaceful and friendly relations now existing between their peoples may be perpetuated;

Convinced that all changes in their relations with one another should be sought only by pacific means and be the result of a peaceful and orderly process, and that any signatory Power which shall hereafter seek to promote its national interests by resort to war should be denied the benefits furnished by this Treaty;

Hopeful that, encouraged by their example, all the other nations of the world will join in this humane endeavor and by adhering to the present Treaty as soon as it comes into force bring their peoples within the scope of its beneficent provisions, thus uniting the civilized nations of the world in a common renunciation of war as an instrument of their national policy;

Have decided to conclude a Treaty and for that purpose have appointed . . . their respective Plenipotentiaries . . . who, having communicated to one another their full powers found in good and due form have agreed upon the following articles:

ARTICLE I: The High Contracting Parties solemnly declare in the names of their respective peoples that they condemn recourse to war for the solution of international controversies, and renounce it as an instrument of national policy in their relations with one another.

ARTICLE II: The High Contracting Parties agree that the settlement or solution of all disputes or conflicts of whatever nature or of whatever origin they may be, which may arise among them, shall never be sought except by pacific means.

ARTICLE III: The present Treaty shall be ratified by the High Contracting Parties named in the Preamble in accordance with their constitutional requirements, and shall take effect as between them as soon as all their several instruments of ratification shall have been deposited at Washington.

This Treaty shall, when it has come into effect as prescribed in the preceding paragraph, remain open as long as may be necessary for adherence by all the other Powers of the world.

# II

## SENATE RATIFICATION

The Senate ratified the Kellogg-Briand Treaty on January 15, 1929, by a vote of 85 to 1 with 9 absent. Despite the overwhelming vote for the treaty, there had been much debate on the issue before the treaty was approved. The following selection is an editorial from *The New Republic* in which both sides of the question were discussed. □ "The Future of the Kellogg Pact." New York: *The New Republic*, Volume 57, Number 731, December 5, 1928, pp. 56-57. Reprinted by permission of *The New Republic*, copyright 1928, Harrison-Blaine of New Jersey, Inc.

It is none too soon . . . to seek to envisage the changes which will be created when the treaty has come into force. If it be examined with a hostile eye, it is seen to be technically one of the weakest and vaguest international instruments ever executed. Mr. Kellogg has insisted that it does not prohibit defensive warfare; but all wars are invariably claimed to be defensive by each participant. It renounces the use of war "as an instrument of national policy," but whatever may be the facts, this is also something of which no nation will admit that it has been guilty. The treaty, by inference, condemns an aggressor nation, but it does not define aggression, nor suggest any machinery by which the facts shall be examined and judgment passed. . . . The British reservation is a gaping hole in the treaty's net; and our own Monroe Doctrine is likely to prove another. What, for instance, is to be said of our landing troops and taking possession of a country, as we have done in Haiti and Nicaragua? To us, this is not war; it is merely the exercise of police power "for the protection of foreign lives and property"; but Latin America might easily take a different view of it, and assert that we had violated the treaty.

It is clear, then, that the treaty will be useful not in any technical and legal sense, but for its general effect upon the moral tone of international relations. Like the League, it will not be strong enough to stop any war between two important powers; it will only be useful in helping to prevent the beginning of hostilities. In this latter role, however, it may easily prove to be of the greatest possible value. For the first time in history, the voice of the jingo will be muffled. Always, in the past, he has been able to set up his shrill, hysterical cry without serious opposition; indeed, anyone who sought to say anything else, in a time of international tension, could be silenced, and usually has been, by the cry of "Traitor!" Whether there is trouble in prospect or not, the militarist who wants his country to possess the biggest army and navy in the world will find that the treaty's terms put him under some embarrassment. No doubt he will surmount it; the sort of person who undertakes this sort of propaganda is usually an insensitive soul in the first place; but at least, his opponents will for the first time be able to support their position by an appeal to the solemnly pledged honor of their country.

The treaty will have value for another reason, which applies to the United States in particular. It will make the necessity for some alternative to the war system so apparent, that it will drive us into efforts toward conciliation and arbitration at a much faster pace than we should voluntarily assume. The changed attitude toward the World Court evinced by President Coolidge and some other persons, is probably a first fruit of the treaty. Despite Mr. Kellogg's explicit disavowal of the possibility, it seems certain that it will bring us to some sort of *modus operandi* with the League in case of a boycott by that body, directed toward a nation deemed guilty, under the Covenant, of aggressive warfare.

The changes which the treaty will bring about in the moral landscape are quite as apparent to its enemies as to its friends; and we may expect a vigorous attempt to prevent ratification. . . . Even if the treaty were of negligible value, failure to adopt it would have an effect upon world opinion, and upon the future of anti-war efforts, which would spell disaster for a generation.

The following reading is excerpted from a speech by Democratic Senator William C. Bruce of Maryland. His view on the effectiveness of the treaty was shared by many other Senators. ☐ *Congressional Record,* 70th Congress, 2nd Session, January 8, 1929, pp. 1332-1333.

I had said that one view that might reasonably be entertained about it was that it was . . . a mere pompous gesture, and that idea I endeavored to expound as effectively as I could. This morning I desire to take up two other views that might reasonably be formed about it.

One view is that it is even worse than a mere parchment futility, because its tendency is to lull our people into a false sense of national security and to lead them to believe that paper professions and promises can take the place of adequate naval and military defenses. In other words, it may be forcibly argued that the tendency of all sanctionless pacts, such as the Kellogg pact, is to create the impression that there is no need for a nation to rely upon the strong hands and stout hearts of its people and adequate preparation in the form of military and naval armaments for its safety . . . . It fosters the feeling in the bosoms of a large element of the population of the United States, . . . that to secure international peace all that it is necessary for us to do is to see to it that sermons, Sunday school lectures, and parlor or pink-tea addresses are delivered from time to time picturing the benevolent aspects and the blessings of peace; in other words, . . . this pact tends to develop the idea that peace can be secured by merely donning white robes, wings, and pious aureoles and crying incessantly, "Peace, peace, perfect peace." . . .

. . . Surely the last World War is not so remote that we do not recall what a "lunatic fringe," to use the graphic phrase of Theodore Roosevelt, of imbecile pacifism, we had to brush aside before we could get down with our allies to the task of preserving the liberties and the civilization of the world. That such a lunatic fringe as that exists to-day can not for a moment be denied. . . .

. . . I propose to vote for the ratification of the Kellogg pact because I agree with the statesmen of England and other European statesmen in believing that it at least measurably tends to draw our country into the only two institutions in the world to-day that hold out any real promise of international peace—that is to say, the World Court and the League of Nations.

Republican Senator William E. Borah of Idaho led the fight for ratification in the Senate. The following reading is excerpted from a speech in which he defended the treaty. □ *Congressional Record,* 70th Congress, 2nd Session, January 15, 1929, p. 1728.

When we come to analyze this treaty, and to consider what the treaty is and what is behind it, and compare it with what is in other treaties for peace and what is behind other treaties, why should this treaty be considered as impractical or as an ideal beyond the power of men and women to attain? Why should a treaty renouncing war and pledging nations to the settlement of their controversies through pacific means be regarded as without value? Is the obligation in this treaty any less binding than the obligation in any other treaty? Is the honor or the good faith of the nations signatory to this treaty any less binding than the honor and the good faith of the nations signatory to any other treaty? If I understand international affairs, there is nothing behind any treaty save the honor and the good faith of the nations signing the treaty. They all rest upon the honor and the faith of the nations, and nothing more.

# III

## HOW DID IT WORK?

When the Japanese invaded Manchuria in September 1931, Secretary of State Henry L. Stimson tried to apply the Kellogg-Briand Treaty to a settlement. Historian Robert Osgood analyzed the effectiveness of the treaty for dealing with the situation. □ Reprinted from *Ideals and Self-Interest in America's Foreign Relations* by Robert Endicott Osgood by permission of The University of Chicago Press, pp. 350, 353-356. Copyright 1953 by The University of Chicago Press.

The Pact of Paris was a self-denying pledge, which asked nothing of its signatories except that they recognize the moral principle of renouncing war as an instrument of national policy and as a means of settling disputes. The Washington Treaties contained specific political and military agreements which bound the contracting powers to observe the terms of a balance of power in the Far East. On the night of September 18, 1931, Japanese armies began overrunning southern Manchuria. This "Manchurian Incident," as the Japanese chose to call it, was a direct challenge to the Pact of Paris and the Washington Treaties; as such it presented the United States with both a moral and a political problem. . . .

Secretary of State Henry L. Stimson took the lead in shaping American policy toward Japan's incursions in Manchuria. He rapidly made up his mind that Japan was chiefly responsible for this disturbance, that she had violated the Kellogg-Briand Pact and the Nine Power Treaty, and that this situation was a vital concern of all the major signatories of these treaties, including the United States. In his view the United States was concerned because its self-interest was involved and because basic moral principles were at stake.

As for America's self-interest, Stimson foresaw Japanese militarism causing direct damage to American trade in China; but more important in his mind than any immediate damage to American trade was the damage to American prestige; for it was his conviction that, ultimately, all of America's material interests in this region, present and future, depended upon the prestige which the United States enjoyed by virtue of its traditional support of China's territorial and administrative integrity. Like so many American missionaries, traders, and statesmen since the dawn of America's interest in the Orient, Stimson was profoundly moved by a vision of a potentially united, powerful, peace-loving, democratic China acting as a dominant, stabilizing influence in the whole Far East and transacting a huge trade with its historic friend and protector, the United States. He held that the United States could not afford to abandon Chinese sovereignty and independence to Japanese aggression and exploitation, for if America lost China's friendship or if China were dominated by a militaristic and aggressive regime or converted into such a regime by Japanese exploitation, the whole future of the United States in the Far East would be ruined. Moreover, he believed that there was a distinct possibility that a struggle between China and Japan might not only destroy America's potentially profitable relations with China but even endanger America's territorial possessions. . . .

Stimson was not willing to base American policy on any narrow, immediate national interest, such as the protection of commercial rights, when great moral issues were at stake. He saw Japan's attack upon China primarily as a sin against international order and stability, as a denial of the theory of the Kellogg Pact and a blow at the whole postwar treaty structure. He believed that Japan was thereby striking at the foundation of a system of collective security, upon which, ultimately, the enlightened self-interest of the United States and all other nations depended. Stimson's convictions about the immorality of Japan's actions gained poignancy by virtue of his strong sympathy for the Chinese people and China's ancient culture, which he regarded as the only firm basis in the Orient for the development of the ideals of Christian civilization.

The principal method which Secretary Stimson employed for dealing with Japan's international sin was collective condemnation backed by the moral force of world opinion. To this end he enunciated a policy of diplomatic nonrecognition. On January 7, 1932, he addressed an identic note to Japan and China stating, with reference to Japan's action in Manchuria, that the United States "does not intend to recognize any situation, treaty, or agreement which may be brought about by means contrary to the covenants and obligations of the Pact of Paris."

Stimson, who, like Hay, regarded co-operation with Great Britain as the touchstone of America's foreign policy, was unsuccessful in his efforts to get the British Foreign Office to take a similar stand, but he did not give up hope of securing parallel action. When Japanese troops clashed with Chinese forces at Shanghai, where British interests were far greater than in Manchuria, he was instrumental in arranging parallel American and British protests to Japan. These protests, combined with surprising Chinese resistance, may have helped induce Japan to withdraw from Shanghai; to Stimson, at any rate, this eventuality was proof of Anglo-American co-operation and world opinion.

He was unable to follow up this success with a joint British and American representation to Japan in terms of the Nine Power Treaty, but on February 23, 1932, after the Japanese had launched a major attack, he decided to deliver another unilateral protest, this time by means of a letter to Senator Borah. In this letter he reviewed the history of the Open Door policy, reaffirmed the Nine Power Treaty and the Kellogg-Briand Pact, declared that the United States would stand by these treaties, called attention to his previous proclamation of the nonrecognition doctrine, and invited the nations of the world to follow that example. Eventually, this vigorous moral stand received something of the color of the collective condemnation Stimson had always sought when, in March, 1932, the League of Nations Assembly unanimously adopted a resolution which incorporated almost verbatim his nonrecognition doctrine.

The position Stimson set forth in his original nonrecognition note and in his letter to Borah became the basis of American policy toward Japan right down to Pearl Harbor. Later—too late, in fact—Franklin Roosevelt's administration combined this policy with restrictions on the export of certain materials essential to the Japanese war effort; and, at the last moment, it froze Japanese assets in the United States, thereby virtually cutting off all exports to Japan. But these measures, coming at a time when Japanese imperialism had gone too far to stop or withdraw, only hastened the blow that began the Pacific war. Before the American government resorted to these last-ditch measures it consistently eschewed the imposition of sanctions against Japan. It resisted public pressure to restrict the export of oil, scrap iron, and other materials which sustained the Japanese military machine. It scrupulously avoided political commitments with other nations and even refused requests from China, Great Britain, and France to act as a mediator. The most that it would contribute toward collective action was to refrain from interfering with measures that other nations might take.

In dealing with Japanese expansion in the 1930's the United States relied upon mobilizing the moral force of nations through collective condemnation. Therefore, the success of American policy depended, largely, upon the effectiveness of constant reiterations of principle and a succession of earnest remonstrances. In retrospect it would seem that this combination of moral chastisement and the rejection of any commitment to coercion or collective action was the most ineffective means possible for achieving the desired end. It did not strengthen any treaties or vindicate international morality; it did not protect America's interests in the Far East; it did not avoid war. It actually worked to defeat all these objectives by arousing Japanese resentment, fixing conditions for a settlement which the Japanese could never meet, and, at the same time, displaying a weakness which encouraged the radical elements in Japan to pursue their imperialist ambitions.

PROBLEM **10**

Isolation and the National Interest

Italy invaded Ethiopia in 1935. The Spanish Civil War broke out in 1936. Although other foreign powers soon intervened in both conflicts, the United States took measures to avoid involvement. The Neutrality Acts of 1935 and 1937 prohibited the exportation of arms and implements of war to any belligerent nation or faction in a civil war.

Some people thought that the policy of neutrality, by avoiding the question of American involvement in war, did nothing to actively prevent it. But most Americans favored neutrality. They felt, despite the development of international commercial aviation, that they were safely distant from Europe and Asia and invulnerable to foreign attack. Furthermore, Americans were preoccupied with resolving the depression of the 1930's and had little interest in foreign involvement. This attitude was strengthened by the Senate Munitions Investigating Committee, under the chairmanship of Senator Gerald P. Nye of South Dakota: in 1934 this committee came to the conclusion that financiers and munitions makers, greedy for profits, had steered the United States into World War I. Americans did not want to be led into a second war by the so-called "merchants of death."

In Europe and Asia, naked aggression continued. Hitler defied the Versailles Treaty by re-occupying in 1936 the demilitarized Rhineland and by absorbing Austria in 1938. He then dismembered Czechoslovakia, later incorporating most of it into Germany. In 1937 Japan renewed the warfare in China which it had begun in 1931. These actions underlined the potential threat of the Rome-Berlin-Tokyo Axis, which, while initiated by Germany and Italy in October 1936, included Japan by November of that year. Officially an agreement to combat Communism, it became in fact an alliance of dictatorships determined upon expansion.

President Franklin D. Roosevelt warned, "Let no one imagine that America will escape, that America can expect mercy." Yet United States public opinion remained divided and did not consistently support any one foreign policy program. Some groups supported an isolationist policy for the Western Hemisphere; others saw no danger to United States interests from Germany, Italy, or Japan; still others favored active resistance to further Axis aggression, even at the risk of involving the United States.

As you read, consider the following questions:

1    What effect did the Neutrality Act of 1937 have on traditional United States policy regarding its neutral rights?

2    Compare the opinions of the four men who debated the question of lifting the arms embargo. On what major points did they agree? On what points did they disagree?

3    How would Lindbergh and the *Times* suggest defending the United States in the event of German aggression across the Atlantic?

4    Compare the arguments favoring neutrality with those favoring revision of the Neutrality Act or intervention on the Allied side. Which alternative do you think was the better one? Why?

# I

### NEUTRALITY ACT, 1937

The Neutrality Act of 1937 lessened the restrictions established by the 1935 Act, which prohibited any trade in munitions with the belligerents. The 1937 Act, portions of which constitute the following reading, permitted "cash and carry" by belligerent nations wanting to purchase non-military materials from the United States. □ "The United States and World Organization During 1936," *International Conciliation* No. 331 (1937). Reprinted by permission of Carnegie Endowment for International Peace.

SECTION I. (a) Whenever the President shall find that there exists a state of war between, or among, two or more foreign States, the President shall proclaim such fact, and it shall thereafter be unlawful to export, or attempt to export, or cause to be exported, arms, ammunition, or implements of war from any place in the United States to any belligerent State named in such proclamation, or to any neutral State for transshipment to, or for the use of, any such belligerent State. . . .

[SEC. 2.] (b) Whenever the President shall have issued a proclamation under the authority of section I of this Act and he shall thereafter find that the placing of restrictions on the shipment of certain articles or materials in addition to arms, ammunition, and implements of war from the United States to belligerent States or to a State wherein civil strife exists, is necessary to promote the security or preserve the peace of the United States or to protect the lives of citizens of the United States, he shall proclaim, and it shall thereafter be unlawful . . . to export or transport . . . to any belligerent State . . . or to any neutral State for transshipment to, or for the use of, any such belligerent State or any such State wherein civil strife exists, any articles or materials whatever until all right, title, and interest therein shall have been transferred to some foreign government, agency, institution, association, partnership, corporation, or national.

# II

## DEBATING THE ARMS EMBARGO

The "cash and carry" clause of the Neutrality Act of 1937 expired on May 1, 1939. President Roosevelt wanted Congress to extend it, but action was withheld until the next regular session of Congress. After war broke out in Europe in September 1939, the President again requested that Congress lift the arms embargo. Debate continued until early November, when Congress voted to lift it, 55 to 24 in the Senate; 243 to 172 in the House. The following excerpt is from a speech which Senator Robert A. Taft of Ohio made on September 6, 1939 in support of the President's proposal.  □ Washington, D.C.: Congressional Digest, Volume 18, Number 10, October 1939, pp. 244-245.

What are the arguments made for our entrance into the war? In the first place, it is said that we cannot stay out. Of course, that is no argument. There is a strong taint of defeatism about it. My own conviction is that we can stay out, but that the only way that we can stay out is to be determined that we will stay out. Neutrality has been the traditional policy of this country for 150 years so far as European disputes are concerned. Any other policy would have involved us in constant war. . . .

Secondly, it has been widely argued that we should enter the war to defend democracy against dictatorship. The President himself, less than a year ago, suggested that it was our duty to defend religion, democracy, and good faith throughout the world, although he proposed methods short of war. I question the whole theory that our entrance into war will preserve democracy. The purpose of the World War was to save democracy, but the actual result destroyed more democracies and set up more dictatorships than the world had seen for many days. We might go in to save England and France and find that, when the war ended, their governments were Communist and Fascist. Nothing is so destructive of forms of government as war. There is real danger to American democracy from our participation in a war. . . .

The third argument that we should enter the war is based on the theory that if France and England are defeated, we will be overwhelmed by Germany. This view is widely held. If it were sound, it would involve the immediate entrance of this country in the war on the side of the English and French and the sending of troops abroad. . . .

Now in the first place I see the possibility of England and France being overwhelmed by Germany, but if that should happen, terrible as the defeat of the English and French would be, there is no reason why it should lead to a German attack on the United States if we have remained neutral. Outrageous as Hitler has been, his ambitions have been based on some logic. It is difficult to say what he would gain by an attack on this country. If by some remote possibility he could overwhelm England and France, it would not end the complications of European policy. England and France defeated Germany but Germany has been a thorn in their side for 20 years. A great people cannot be destroyed. . . .

. . . I believe that the embargo on the shipment of arms, ammunition and implements of war should be repealed on condition that export be permitted only on a cash-and-carry basis. I see nothing unneutral in the shipment of munitions of war to any nation which comes and gets them. The distinction between the shipment of munitions and raw materials, between gun cotton and cotton is sentimental rather than real. The fact that such a policy may be of assistance to England and France at the present moment does not seem to make it less neutral. I have always questioned the wisdom of embargoing the shipment of arms to other nations. If they do not secure those arms from us, they will secure them from other nations or, if the policy is generally adopted, every small nation will have to build up its own munition plants and thus create all the more interest in favor of war.

The following excerpts are from a speech which Republican Senator William E. Borah of Idaho made on October 2, 1939. ☐ *Congressional Record,* 85th Congress, 1st Session, October 2, 1939, pp. 66, 68-69, 73.

... [When] this nation solemnly resolved and wrote into its law that it would never again furnish arms, munitions, and implements of war to any nation engaged in war it was almost universally believed that not only here but abroad we had marked an epoch in the cause of peace, that we had offered a challenge to the reign of force which would in time break its hold on the people of the world. . . .

We are not here today to repeal the embargo law because of any injury it is doing to the people of the United States. We are here seeking to repeal it because certain nations feel that they want the arms and munitions; yet that is the very reason why we passed the law, to see that neither they nor anyone else got them. Is it working? If it were not working, they would not be complaining. It is the fact that it is working that causes the complaint.

We passed this law because we wanted to stay out of European conflicts. Does the sale of arms, munitions, and implements of war tend more to keep us out of European conflicts than the refusal to sell arms? If our arms are not upon the sea, if they are not in the fray, if they are not hurting any one or helping any one, how do they help to bring on war? If they are excluded from all, is not the tendency to keep us out of war?

On September 18, 1939, Democratic Congressman from Virginia Clifton A. Woodrum urged modification of the Neutrality Act. ☐ Washington D.C.: *Congressional Digest,* Volume 18, Number 10, October 1939, pp. 246-247.

I confess I am unable to find much of a convincing nature in the arguments against neutrality revision. Some of our friends seem to suddenly have a bad case of jitters, for fear we will offend someone. Just what might we do to 'get us into war' and with whom? Now, let's be a bit realistic about the matter. Every thoughtful citizen knows full well that the continued peace and security of our own country, and our ability to stay out of war, may to a very large extent depend upon the outcome of the present conflict in Europe and Asia. What are we supposed to do? Pull down the shades, turn out the lights, and crawl under the bed? Is it possible that there are those amongst us who are so credulous as believe that the German Dictator entertains any regard for the American Government, or that he would hesitate a split instant to take any action of any sort against America or her interests if he thought it would serve his purpose? Must we not know that if the time ever comes that Germany or her allies wish to mix it with America — and such time will most likely never come — that it will make no earthly difference whether we have sold supplies to belligerents? Or what our attitude has been? Does not the record show that to Herr Hitler international law means nothing? Treaties mere scraps of paper? And that his will is superior to the laws of man or God? As Great Britain and France have vividly realized, the only thing that will stop him is superior force; let us not emulate the stupidity of the ostrich and seek to avoid facing the coming storm by burying our heads in the sand. . . .

Now let us remember right at this point that it oftentimes happens that a belligerent nation, because of economic conditions or geographic location may reap very great benefit from the neutrality of another nation. . . . Under our so-called Neutrality Act as it stands today, Germany is very decidedly and definitely favored. For economic and geographic reasons, Germany would not likely — under any circumstances — want American planes, but Great Britain, France, and Canada have now unfilled orders in America for airplanes and other defense implements. Our so-called present neutrality denies to these nations the right to purchase these necessary implements of war. Now, where does this lead us? Germany has rushed headlong into this war, after years of feverish preparations. Nothing could stop her. It was forced upon Great Britain and France. They have tried in every conceivable way to promote peace and to avoid war. They have not spent their time and energy in building up a huge war machine, as has Germany. Our present so-called neutrality, which denies these democracies the right to buy our supplies, is a most flagrant and unjust discrimination against these democracies and in favor of the aggressor in this sorry business. It just doesn't make sense.

What do we propose to do if the law is amended?

We propose, as I have said, to say to all of the belligerent nations that they may purchase our commodities in America for cash, but that they must load them upon their own ships and be responsible for their transportation to their own countries. There is no way that such a policy can involve us with any other belligerent nation.

Democratic Senator David I. Walsh of Massachusetts spoke in favor of the Neutrality Law on July 4, 1939. ☐ Washington, D.C.: Congressional Digest, Volume 18, Number 10, October 1939, p. 253.

It is certain, if anything is certain, that a world bristling with national enmities, a world divided into two war-like groups, can be no menace to us while we remain definitely neutral. We ought to do this for no other reason than that, if all the rest of the world crumbles, we shall preserve for humanity a haven of safety, containing all the elements on which we may continue to build a prosperous democracy.

A strictly neutral attitude does not imply a selfish concern with our own affairs or refusal to assume our part in the common burdens of humanity. That is always the argument advanced by those who wish us to share in their burdens. A strong neutral position will enable America to do more for humanity in general than an America growing rich through selling arms and munitions to belligerents, thereby arousing the hatred of those to whom we are unable to make sales of arms and munitions, and, after the war, with almost certainty, being plunged into another and greater depression.

Another important consideration which should prompt us to strict neutrality is the possibility that, should the United States join in another war, it would result in the end of American democracy and the rise of a totalitarian state.

In the light of these facts I am opposed to repeal of the existing ban on exports of munitions of war in time of war to nations at war. The provisions of the present Neutrality Act in this respect, in my judgment, are an essential element of any policy of real neutrality, and that is the kind of neutrality that the American people desire and ought to have.

# III

## U.S. SUPPORT FOR BRITAIN

By the middle of 1940, after Poland, Denmark, Holland, Belgium, Luxembourg, and France had fallen to German occupation, Britain was threatened with invasion. President Roosevelt negotiated with Prime Minister Winston Churchill the exchange of fifty overage destroyers for eight sites for American naval and military bases on British territory from Newfoundland to British Guiana. Congress carried the country even deeper into probable involvement by the Lend-Lease Act of March 1941, which authorized the transfer of war equipment to "any country whose defense the President deems vital to the defense of the United States." These actions placed the United States squarely behind Britain and the victims of Axis aggression, from France to China. The decision to risk involvement had been made.

The America First Committee, organized to support isolationism and pacifism in 1940, claimed an influential member in Charles A. Lindbergh, the noted aviator. The following reading is excerpted from a speech which Lindbergh made in April 1941. ☐ *The New York Times,* April 24, 1941, p. 12. Copyright 1941 by The New York Times Company. Reprinted by permission.

We are no better prepared today than France was when the interventionists in Europe persuaded her to attack the Siegfried Line. . . .

. . . I opposed this war before it was declared, and . . . I have constantly advocated a negotiated peace. I did not feel that England and France had a reasonable chance of winning. France has now been defeated; and, despite the propaganda and confusion of recent months, it is now obvious that England is losing the war. I believe this is realized even by the British Government. But they have one last desperate plan remaining. They hope that they may be able to persuade us to send another American Expeditionary Force to Europe, and to share with England militarily, as well as financially, the fiasco of this war. . . .

. . . When England asks us to enter this war, she is considering her own future, and that of her empire. In making our reply, I believe we should consider the future of the United States and that of the Western Hemisphere. . . .

. . . . I have been forced to the conclusion that we cannot win this war for England, regardless of how much assistance we extend.

I ask you to look at the map of Europe today and see if you can suggest any way in which we could win this war if we entered it. Suppose we had a large army in America, trained and equipped. Where would we send it to fight? The campaigns of the war show only too clearly how difficult it is to force a landing, or to maintain an army, on a hostile coast.

Suppose we took our Navy from the Pacific, and used it to convoy British shipping. That would not win the war for England. It would, at best, permit her to exist under the constant bombing of the German air fleet. Suppose we had an air force that we could send to Europe. Where could it operate? Some of our squadrons might be based in the British Isles; but it is physically impossible to base enough aircraft in the British

Isles alone to equal in strength the aircraft that can be based on the Continent of Europe. . . .

When these facts are cited, the interventionists shout that we are defeatists, that we are undermining the principles of democracy, and that we are giving comfort to Germany by talking about our military weakness. . . .

I say it is the interventionist in America, as it was in England and in France, who gives comfort to the enemy. I say it is they who are undermining the principles of democracy when they demand that we take a course to which more than 80 per cent of our citizens are opposed. I charge them with being the real defeatists, for their policy has led to the defeat of every country that followed their advice since this war began. . . .

When history is written, the responsibility for the downfall of the democracies of Europe will rest squarely upon the shoulders of the interventionists who led their nations into war uninformed and unprepared. With their shouts of defeatism, and their disdain of reality, they have already sent countless thousands of young men to death in Europe. . . .

. . . There is a policy open to this nation that will lead to success — a policy that leaves us free to follow our own way of life, and to develop our own civilization. . . . It was incorporated in the Monroe Doctrine. . . . It recommends the maintenance of armed forces sufficient to defend this hemisphere from attack by any combination of foreign powers. It demands faith in an independent American destiny. This is the policy of the America First Committee today. It is a policy not of isolation, but of independence; not of defeat, but of courage.

The New York Times answered Lindbergh in an editorial later that month. □ The New York Times, April 30, 1941, p. 18. Copyright 1941 by The New York Times Company. Reprinted by permission.

It has been said, times without number, that if Hitler cannot cross the English Channel he cannot cross three thousand miles of sea. But there is only one reason why he has not crossed the English Channel. That is because forty-five million determined Britons in a heroic resistance have converted their island into an armed base from which proceeds a steady stream of sea and air power. As Secretary Hull has said: "It is not the water that bars the way. It is the resolute determination of British arms. Were the control of the seas by Britain lost, the Atlantic would no longer be an obstacle—rather, it would become a broad highway for a conqueror moving westward." . . .

. . . We shall be in deadly danger the moment British sea power fails; the moment the eastern gates of the Atlantic are open to the aggressor; the moment we are compelled to divide our one-ocean Navy between two oceans simultaneously.

. . . The master of Europe will have at his command shipways that can outbuild us, the resources of twenty conquered nations to furnish his materials, the oil of the Middle East to stoke his engines, the slave labor of a continent—bound by no union rules, and not working on a forty-hour week—to turn out his production.

Grant Hitler the gigantic prestige of a victory over Britain, and who can doubt that the first result, on our side of the ocean, would be the prompt appearance of imitation Nazi regimes in a half-dozen Latin-American nations, forced to be on the winning side, begging favors, clamoring for admission to the Axis? . . .

. . . With Britain gone, . . . with all hope of resurrection denied to the little democracies that have contributed so generously to our civilization and our culture, with the hobnailed boots of an ignorant and obscene barbarism echoing in every capital from London to Athens, we should live in a new world, changed beyond all recognition. . . .

. . . Our confidence would be undermined, our vision dimmed, our ranks divided. In a dark, uncertain world we should stand alone, deriving from no other country the sustaining strength of a common faith in our democratic institutions.

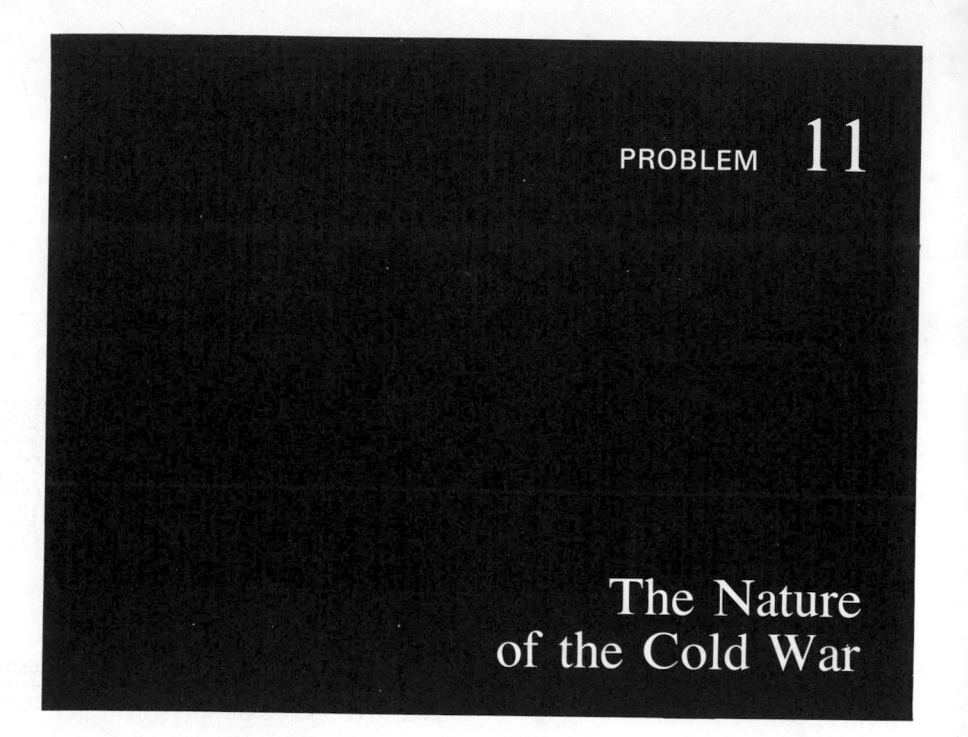

PROBLEM **11**

The Nature
of the Cold War

At the end of World War II the pre-war distribution of power had changed dramatically. Germany, Italy, and Japan had been defeated and occupied. Britain and France had been physically and economically exhausted. Western Europe was a "power vacuum" of nations unable to resist pressures which either the United States or the Soviet Union could exert upon them. The United States remained physically and economically the most powerful nation in the world. The Soviet Union had developed great economic strength during the war and had increased its land area by absorbing Estonia, Latvia, and Lithuania. The United States and the Soviet Union held positions of such strength that each one would inevitably play a prominent role in determining the future.

Although the United States and the Soviet Union were fundamentally opposed in political and economic ideologies, they had fought together against Germany in the war. After the fighting ended, they cooperated in the treaty talks and in establishing the United Nations. Many people began to overlook the differences in ideology, which had fostered mutual suspicion before World War II, and to believe that this cooperative attitude was the way to world peace.

But the expansionist nature of Soviet policy soon became clear. While Western nations were disarming in 1946, Communist party leader Joseph Stalin declared a new Five-Year Plan to enlarge Soviet military operations. In 1947 the Soviet government created the Cominform. Replacing the Comintern, which had been discontinued in 1943, it became the Communist propaganda organization. Between 1945 and 1948 Communist regimes were imposed on Rumania, Bulgaria, Poland, Hungary, Albania, and Czechoslovakia.

American policy shifted from a wartime attitude of cooperation to one of clear opposition. The intense rivalry which grew out of this opposition never provoked open war, but it became known as the "Cold War." The United States faced the problem of reacting to a new kind of rival which wanted to pursue the struggle for world dominance.

As you read, consider the following questions:

1    What actions by the Soviet Union contributed to American suspicion of Russian intentions? Do you think that the United States interpreted Russian intentions correctly?

2    How did Churchill characterize the Soviet Union? What policy was he asking the United States to adopt? On what grounds did he urge this policy?

3    What arguments did Wallace offer to explain Soviet suspicions of American intentions? Was his reasoning valid? Why?

4    Which assessment of the Soviet Union do you think was the more accurate, Churchill's or Wallace's? Why?

5    How did the policy of containment attempt to deal with the intense rivalry between the United States and the Soviet Union? Do you think that Kennan was right or wrong in not proposing an immediate solution to the Cold War? Why?

# I

## THE NEW PRESSURE OF SOVIET POWER

The weakened condition of Europe and the rapid demobilization of the United States Army encouraged Soviet ambitions for expansion. Historian John Spanier described the international situation that developed in the first year after the war and defined three immediate courses of action open to the United States.    □ John W. Spanier, *American Foreign Policy Since World War II*, pp. 19-26. 2nd edn. New York: Frederick A. Praeger, Inc., copyright © 1962; London: Pall Mall Press, 1962.

The American dream of postwar peace and Big Three [Britain, Soviet Union, United States] cooperation was to be shattered as the Soviet Union expanded into Eastern and Central Europe, imposing its control upon Poland, Hungary, Bulgaria, Romania, and Albania. (Yugoslavia was already under the Communist control of Marshal Tito, and Czechoslovakia was living under the shadow of the Red Army.) In each of these nations of Eastern Europe where the Russians had their troops, they unilaterally established pro-Soviet coalition governments. The key post in these regions — the ministry of the interior, which usually controlled the police — was in the hands of the Communists. With this decisive lever of power in their grasp, it was an easy matter to extend their domination and subvert the independence of these countries. Thus, as the war drew to a close, it became clear that the words of the Yalta Declaration, in which the Russians had committed themselves to free elections and democratic governments in Eastern Europe, meant quite different things to the Russians than to Americans. To the Russians, "democratic governments" meant Communist governments, and "free elections" meant elections from which parties not favorable to the Communists were barred. . . .

Greece, Turkey, and Iran were the first states beyond the confines of the Red Army to feel the resulting expansionist pressure of the Soviet Union. . . .

The pressure on Iran began in early 1946 when the Russians refused to withdraw their troops from that country. These troops had been there since late 1941, when Russia and Britain had invaded Iran in order to forestall increased Nazi influence and to use Iran as a corridor for the transportation of military aid shipped by the West to the Persian Gulf for transit to Russia. The Russians had occupied northern Iran, the British the central and southern sections. The Tripartite Treaty of Alliance signed in early 1942 by Iran, Britain, and Russia specified that within six months of the cessation of hostilities all troops would be withdrawn; the Allies also pledged themselves to respect Iran's sovereignty and territorial and political independence.

The final date set for evacuation from Iran was March 2, 1946. British and United States troops — the latter had arrived after America's entry into the war, to help move the lend-lease supplies to Russia — had already left. Only the Soviet troops still remained. Indeed, the Russians were sending in more troops and tanks. Their goal: to reduce Iran to a Soviet satellite. The Russians had, in fact, begun their campaign in late 1944, when they demanded exclusive mineral and oil rights in northern

Iran and offered to supply the Iranians with experts to help administer their government. When the Iranian Government rejected these demands, the Russians had organized a revolt by the Communist-controlled Tudeh Party in the north. The revolt began openly in November, 1945, and the Red Army prevented the Iranian Army from quelling it. The Tudeh Party, renamed the Democratic Party, then formed a government in Azerbaijan. The Russian game was clear: to force the Iranian Government to recognize the Soviet puppet regime in Azerbaijan, which would then send "elected representatives" to the legislature in Teheran. These would then exert pressure on the government to grant Russia the economic and political control it wanted in Iran. The result would have been the conversion of Iran into a Soviet satellite. It was imperative, therefore, that Soviet troops be forced to withdraw. . . .

. . . In August, 1946, the Soviet Union renewed its demand, in a note to the United States and Britain, for a new administration of the Straits. In effect, this would have turned Turkey, like Iran, into a Soviet satellite.

In Greece, too, Communist pressure was exerted on the government through wide-scale guerrilla warfare, which began in the fall of 1946. . . .

. . . If Britain had not helped finance — as well as train and equip — the army and kept troops in the country to stabilize the situation, Greece would in all probability have collapsed. . . .

In all these situations, the American Government was suddenly confronted with the need for action to support Britain, the traditional guardian of this area against encroachment. In the case of Iran, the United States and Britain delivered firm statements which strongly implied that the two countries would use force to defend Iran. The Soviet response in late March, 1946, was the announcement that the Red Army would be withdrawn during the next five to six weeks. In the Turkish case, the United States sent a naval task force into the Mediterranean immediately after the receipt of the Soviet note on August 7. Twelve days later, the United States replied to the note by rejecting the Russian demand to share sole responsibility for the defense of the Straits with Turkey. Britain sent a similar reply. . . . [The] Administration's actions in Iran and Turkey were merely swift reactions to immediate crises. They were not the product of an over-all American strategy. Such a coherent strategy could only arise from a new assessment of Soviet foreign policy. . . .

Three positions became clear during this period. At one extreme stood that old realist Winston Churchill. At the end of the European war, he had counseled against the withdrawal of American troops. He had insisted that they stay, together with British troops, in order to force the Soviet Union to live up to its Yalta obligations regarding free elections in Eastern Europe and the withdrawal of the Red Army from Eastern Germany. . . .

At the other extreme stood Secretary of Commerce Henry Wallace, who felt it was precisely the kind of aggressive attitude expressed by Churchill that was to blame for Soviet hostility. . . .

The American Government and public wavered between these two positions. . . . We have tried to gain Russia's amity by being a friend; it was now up to her leaders to demonstrate a similarly friendly attitude toward us as well. Paper agreements, written in such general terms that they actually hid divergent purposes, were no longer regarded as demonstrating such friendship. Something more than paper agreements was needed: Russian words would have to be matched by Russian deeds. . . .

. . . The . . . American position, as one political analyst has aptly summed it up, "meant to most of its exponents that the Soviet Union had to be induced by firmness to play the game in the American way. There was no consistent official suggestion that the United States should begin to play a different game." The prerequisite for such a suggestion was that American policy-makers recognize the revolutionary nature of the Soviet regime.

# II

## ALTERNATIVE POLICIES FOR THE UNITED STATES

Both Winston Churchill and Henry Wallace defined the Soviet threat and presented solutions to it. The British war leader presented his "Iron Curtain" address at Fulton, Missouri on March 5, 1946 as President Harry Truman listened approvingly. □ Randolph S. Churchill, Editor, *The Sinews of Peace, Post-War Speeches by Winston S. Churchill,* pp. 98, 100-101, 103. London: Cassell and Company Ltd. Boston: Houghton Mifflin Company, copyright 1949.

Neither the sure prevention of war, nor the continuous rise of world organisation will be gained without what I have called the fraternal association of the English-speaking peoples. This means a special relationship between the British Commonwealth and Empire and the United States. . . . It should carry with it the continuance of the present facilities for mutual security by the joint use of all Naval and Air Force bases in the possession of either country all over the world. This would perhaps double the mobility of the American Navy and Air Force. It would greatly expand that of the British Empire Forces and it might well lead, if and as the world calms down, to important financial savings. Already we use together a large number of islands; more may well be entrusted to our joint care in the near future. . . .

A shadow has fallen upon the scenes so lately lighted by the Allied victory. Nobody knows what Soviet Russia and its Communist international organisation intends to do in the immediate future, or what are the limits, if any, to their expansive and proselytising tendencies. . . . It is my duty however, for I am sure you would wish me to state the facts as I see them to you, to place before you certain facts about the present position in Europe.

From Stettin in the Baltic to Trieste in the Adriatic, an iron curtain has descended across the Continent. Behind that line lie all the capitals of the ancient states of Central and Eastern Europe. Warsaw, Berlin, Prague, Vienna, Budapest, Belgrade, Bucharest and Sofia, all these famous cities and the populations around them lie in what I must call the Soviet sphere, and all are subject in one form or another, not only to Soviet influence but to a very high and, in many cases, increasing measure of control from Moscow. . . .

. . . An attempt is being made by the Russians in Berlin to build up a quasi-Communist party in their zone of Occupied Germany by showing special favours to groups of left-wing German leaders. . . .

If now the Soviet Government tries, by separate action, to build up a pro-Communist Germany in their areas, this will cause new serious difficulties in the British and American zones, and will give the defeated Germans the power of putting themselves up to auction between the Soviets and the Western Democracies. Whatever conclusions may be drawn from these facts — and facts they are — this is certainly not the Liberated Europe we fought to build up. Nor is it one which contains the essentials of permanent peace. . . .

From what I have seen of our Russian friends and Allies during the war, I am convinced that there is nothing they admire so much as strength, and there is nothing for which they have less respect than for weakness, especially military weakness. For that reason the old doctrine of a balance of power is unsound. We cannot afford, if we can help it, to work on narrow margins, offering temptations to a trial of strength. If the Western Democracies stand together in strict adherence to the principles of the

United Nations Charter, their influence for furthering those principles will be immense and no one is likely to molest them. If however they become divided or falter in their duty and if these all-important years are allowed to slip away then indeed catastrophe may overwhelm us all.

Secretary of Commerce Wallace presented his views in a letter to President Harry Truman on July 23, 1946. On the basis of this letter Truman asked his Secretary to resign from the cabinet. □ Henry A. Wallace, "The Path to Peace with Russia." New York: *The New Republic,* Volume 115, Number 13, September 30, 1946, pp. 401, 404-406. Reprinted by permission of *The New Republic,* copyright 1946, Harrison-Blaine of New Jersey, Inc.

I have been increasingly disturbed about the trend of international affairs since the end of the war, and I am even more troubled by the apparently growing feeling among the American people that another war is coming and the only way that we can head it off is to arm ourselves to the teeth. Yet all of past history indicates that an armaments race does not lead to peace but to war. The months just ahead may well be the crucial period which will decide whether the civilized world will go down in destruction after the five or ten years needed for several nations to arm themselves with atomic bombs. . . .

. . . [To] the Russians all of the defense and security measures of the Western powers seem to have an aggressive intent. Our actions to expand our military security system — such steps as extending the Monroe Doctrine to include the arming of the Western Hemisphere nations, our present monopoly of the atomic bomb, our interest in outlying bases and our general support of the British Empire — appear to them as going far beyond the requirements of defense. I think we might feel the same if the United States were the only capitalistic country in the world, and the principal socialistic countries were creating a level of armed strength far exceeding anything in their previous history. From the Russian point of view, also, the granting of a loan to Britain and the lack of tangible results on their request to borrow for rehabilitation purposes may be regarded as another evidence of strengthening of an anti-Soviet bloc.

Finally, our resistance to her attempts to obtain warm-water ports and her own security system in the form of "friendly" neighboring states seems, from the Russian point of view, to clinch the case. After twenty-five years of isolation and after having achieved the status of a major power, Russia believes that she is entitled to recognition of her new status. Our interest in establishing democracy in Eastern Europe, where democracy by and large has never existed, seems to her an attempt to re-establish the encirclement of unfriendly neighbors which was created after the last war and which might serve as a springboard of still another effort to destroy her. . . .

The real test lies in the achievement of international unity. It will be fruitless to continue to seek solutions for the many specific problems that face us in the making of the peace and in the establishment of an enduring international order without first achieving an atmosphere of mutual trust and confidence. The task admittedly is not an easy one. . . . But the task is not an insuperable one if we take into account that to other nations our foreign policy consists not only of the principles that we advocate but of the actions we take.

Fundamentally, this comes down to the point . . . that even our own security, in the sense that we have known it in the past, cannot be preserved by military means in a world armed with atomic weapons. The only type of security which can be maintained by our own military force is . . . a security against invasion after all our cities and perhaps forty million of our city population have been destroyed by atomic weapons. . . . It is not the kind of security that our people and the people of the other United Nations are striving for.

# III

## GENESIS OF A NEW POLICY: CONTAINMENT

By mid-1947 the breach between the Western powers and the Soviet Union had widened dramatically. Up to this time the United States had not shown a consistent policy regarding the Soviet Union. In July 1947 George F. Kennan, then chief of policy planning for the State Department, wrote anonymously proposing a new policy.  □ "X," "The Sources of Soviet Conduct." Abridged by special permission from *Foreign Affairs*, July 1947. Copyright by the Council on Foreign Relations, Inc., New York. Volume 25, Number 4, pp. 571-576, 580-582.

Today the major part of the structure of Soviet power is committed to the perfection of the dictatorship and to the maintenance of the concept of Russia as in a state of siege, with the enemy lowering beyond the walls. And the millions of human beings who form that part of the structure of power must defend at all costs this concept of Russia's position, for without it they are themselves superfluous. . . .

... [Stress] has come to be laid primarily on those concepts which relate most specifically to the Soviet régime itself: to its position as the sole truly Socialist régime in a dark and misguided world, and to the relationships of power within it.

The first of these concepts is that of the innate antagonism between capitalism and Socialism. We have seen how deeply that concept has become imbedded in foundations of Soviet power. It has profound implications for Russia's conduct as a member of international society. It means that there can never be on Moscow's side any sincere assumption of a community of aims between the Soviet Union and powers which are regarded as capitalist. It must invariably be assumed in Moscow that the aims of the capitalist world are antagonistic to the Soviet régime, and therefore to the interests of the peoples it controls. . . .

This means that we are going to continue for a long time to find the Russians difficult to deal with. . . . The theory of the inevitability of the eventual fall of capitalism has the fortunate connotation that there is no hurry about it. . . .

. . . Thus the Kremlin has no compunction about retreating in the face of superior force. And being under the compulsion of no timetable, it does not get panicky under the necessity for such retreat. Its political action is a fluid stream which moves constantly, wherever it is permitted to move, toward a given goal. Its main concern is to make sure that it has filled every nook and cranny available to it in the basin of world power. But if it finds unassailable barriers in its path, it accepts these philosophically and accommodates itself to them. The main thing is that there should always be pressure, unceasing constant pressure, toward the desired goal. There is no trace of any feeling in Soviet psychology that that goal must be reached at any given time.

These considerations make Soviet diplomacy at once easier and more difficult to deal with than the diplomacy of individual aggressive leaders like Napoleon and Hitler. On the one hand it is more sensitive to contrary force, more ready to yield on individual sectors of the diplomatic front when that force is felt to be too strong, and thus more rational in the logic and rhetoric of power. On the other hand it cannot be easily defeated or discouraged by a single victory on the part of its opponents. . . .

In these circumstances it is clear that the main element of any United States policy toward the Soviet Union must be that of a long-term, patient but firm and vigilant containment of Russian expansive tendencies. It is important to note, however, that such a policy has nothing to do with . . . threats or blustering or superfluous gestures of outward "toughness."

While the Kremlin is basically flexible in its reaction to political realities, it is by no means unamenable to considerations of prestige. Like almost any other government, it can be placed by tactless and threatening gestures in a position where it cannot afford to yield even though this might be dictated by its sense of realism. The Russian leaders are keen judges of human psychology, and as such they are highly conscious that loss of temper and of self-control is never a source of strength in political affairs. They are quick to exploit such evidences of weakness. For these reasons, it is a *sine qua non* of successful dealing with Russia that the foreign government in question should remain at all times cool and collected and that its demands on Russian policy should be put forward in such a manner as to leave the way open for a compliance not too detrimental to Russian prestige. . . .

It is clear that the United States cannot expect in the foreseeable future to enjoy political intimacy with the Soviet régime. . . . It must continue to expect that Soviet policies will reflect . . . a cautious, persistent pressure toward the disruption and weakening of all rival influence and rival power. . . .

. . . But the United States has it in its power to increase enormously the strains under which Soviet policy must operate, to force upon the Kremlin a far greater degree of moderation and circumspection than it has had to observe in recent years, and in this way to promote tendencies which must eventually find their outlet in either the break-up or the gradual mellowing of Soviet power. . . .

Thus the decision will really fall in large measure in this country itself. The issue of Soviet-American relations is in essence a test of the over-all worth of the United States as a nation among nations. To avoid destruction the United States need only measure up to its own best traditions and prove itself worthy of preservation as a great nation.

PROBLEM 12

Problems of an Alliance

In 1947 the Greek prime minister made an urgent appeal to the United States for assistance against Communist guerrillas and Soviet pressure on the borders of his country. President Harry Truman responded with a new principle of American diplomacy which became known as the Truman Doctrine: "I believe that it must be the policy of the United States to support free peoples who are resisting attempted subjugation by armed minorities or by outside pressures." Truman's message to Congress and the subsequent agreement to provide financial aid and military advice to Turkey as well as Greece were more than assistance; they were the first steps in realizing the policy of containment of the Soviet Union.

It soon became evident that assistance to Greece and Turkey alone could not halt expansionist Communist influence. A devastated and physically exhausted Europe was in dire need of large-scale economic aid. Consequently, the European Recovery Program, or Marshall Plan, was designed to help European nations get back on their feet by their own efforts and with $17 billion of United States assistance. This aid was offered to all European nations, but the Soviet Union refused to permit its satellites to accept it, setting up for them a rival plan.

In 1948 the Cold War deepened. A Communist minority took full power in Czechoslovakia after gaining key offices in a divided government. To the Western nations, strong Communist parties in such countries as France and Italy seemed increasingly menacing. Furthermore, hoping to force Britain, France, and the United States to abandon their sectors of military occupation in West Berlin, the Soviet Union closed Allied land and water routes into the city. The Allies supplied Berlin in a successful airlift of goods, causing the Soviet Union to abandon its eleven-month blockade in May 1949.

These events dramatized the split between East and West and helped turn the Western nations toward close military cooperation to counter the Soviet threat. In March 1948, Britain, France, Belgium, the Netherlands, and Luxembourg signed the Brussels Pact, a fifty-year defensive pact providing for joint military action. In April 1949 the United States signed the North Atlantic Treaty with Britain, France, Belgium, the Netherlands, Luxembourg, Canada, Iceland, Denmark, Norway, Portugal, and Italy. In 1951 Greece and Turkey signed the Treaty, and in 1954 the German Federal Republic (West Germany) signed it. This alliance bound the member nations to a mutual defense plan which would be effective in case of an attack on any one of them by another power. The signatories thought that the best hope of restraining aggression was to warn a potential aggressor that they would retaliate as a unit. Their intention was to contain the Soviet Union within its existing area of control.

The policy with which Truman responded to the Greek prime minister's appeal had grown within two years to include twelve nations. The growth of the idea of containment into a multilateral defense pact presented several major problems. The first problem was in the reaction of the Soviet Union to such a show of strength. Would the Soviet Union check its aggression when faced with the power of the North Atlantic Treaty Organization (NATO)? Would the creation of NATO precipitate an all-out arms race, perhaps making World War III even more likely? A second problem was in the reaction of the member nations to the necessity of cooperating with one another. Would NATO strengthen the Western nations or could one member, acting independently, provoke the Soviet Union to attack and thus threaten the security of the other members?

As you read, consider the following questions:

1    How did acceptance of the North Atlantic Treaty mark a change in the traditional foreign policy of the United States?

**2** Do you think that American adherence to the Treaty meant that the United States distrusted the United Nations? Why?
**3** Why did Connally favor the treaty? Why did Taft oppose it? Which man, do you think, had the more convincing argument?
**4** What were the French criticisms of NATO? Compare Under Secretary Ball's remarks about the alliance with those made by Winckler. How could you characterize French and American national interests from these excerpts?
**5** What did the Western nations hope to accomplish through NATO? Why is the United States strongly supporting NATO despite De Gaulle's attitude toward it?

# I

### WHAT IS NATO?

On March 18, 1966, fourteen member nations of the North Atlantic Treaty Organization simultaneously released a statement defining NATO and endorsing their participation in it. The following reading is the text of that statement. □ "14 NATO Nations Declare Alliance Essential to Common Security." Washington, D.C.: *Department of State Bulletin*, Volume 54, Number 1397, April 4, 1966, p. 536.

The following declaration has been agreed between the Heads of Governments of Belgium, Canada, Denmark, Federal Republic of Germany, Greece, Iceland, Italy, Luxembourg, the Netherlands, Norway, Portugal, Turkey, the United Kingdom, and the United States.

The North Atlantic Treaty and the organization established under it are both alike essential to the security of our countries.

The Atlantic Alliance has ensured its efficacy as an instrument of defense and deterrence by the maintenance in peacetime of an integrated and interdependent military organization in which, as in no previous alliance in history, the efforts and resources of each are combined for the common security of all. We are convinced that this organization is essential and will continue. No system of bilateral arrangements can be a substitute.

The North Atlantic Treaty and the organization are not merely instruments of the common defense. They meet a common political need and reflect the readiness and determination of the member countries of the North Atlantic community to consult and act together wherever

possible in the safeguard of their freedom and security and in the furtherance of international peace, progress and prosperity.

# II

## CONTAINMENT OR PROVOCATION?

Texas Democrat Tom Connally, chairman of the Senate Committee on Foreign
Relations, enjoyed an influential position. The following reading is an excerpt from Connally's address to the Senate on July 5, 1949, in which he urged
passage of the treaty. □ *Congressional Record*, 81st Congress, 1st Session,
July 5, 1949, p. 8818.

It is obvious that the United States gains much by declaring now,
in this written pact, the course of action we would follow even if the
treaty did not exist. Without a treaty, we were drawn into two world
wars to preserve the security of the North Atlantic community. Can anyone doubt that we would become involved in a third world conflict if it
should ever come?

After the United States is involved in war, it cooperates with and
coordinates its activities with its allies. A joint enterprise to win the
war and defend its cause in union with its associates is launched with
all of its power and might. If it is wise and desirable to cooperate with
our partners after we shall have been involved in a war, why should it
be wrong or unwise to cooperate with them prior to the outbreak of war
for the purpose of preventing war?

From now on, no one will misread our motives or underestimate our
determination to stand in defense of our freedom. By letting the world
know exactly where we stand, we erect a fundamental policy that out-
lasts the daily fluctuations of diplomacy, and the twists and turns of
psychological warfare which the Soviet Union has chosen to wage against
us. This public preview of our intentions has a steadying effect upon the
course of human events both at home, where our people want no more
Normandy beachheads, and abroad, where men must work and live in the
sinister shadow of aggression.

The treaty, in thus encouraging a feeling of confidence and security, will provide an atmosphere in which the European recovery program
can move forward with new vitality. We know that encouraging progress
has already been made. We know, too, that momentum of confidence has
been building up in Europe as a direct result of our assistance.

But that is not enough. The greatest obstacle that stands in the way of complete recovery is the pervading and paralyzing sense of insecurity. The treaty is a powerful antidote to this poison. It will go far in dispelling the fear that has plagued Europe since the war.

With this protection afforded by the Atlantic Pact, western Europe can breathe easier again. It can plan its future with renewed hope. New business enterprises, increased trade, and planning for long-range recovery should be the direct results.

The treaty is thus a logical and necessary complement to the recovery program. Through it we shall protect our past and future investments in that famous calculated risk which already has paid remarkable dividends. We might even look forward to the time when we can anticipate rather substantial savings in our ECA [Economic Cooperation Administration, which administered Marshall Plan aid] expenditures, once the full impact of the treaty has been felt in Europe.

The strongest and most eloquent opponent of administration policies in the Senate was Ohio Republican, Robert A. Taft. In the following reading, an excerpt from a speech to the Senate, Taft warned of possible dangers in the North Atlantic treaty. Republican Taft was a conservative, and his stand on the treaty was consistent with his political philosophy. □ *Congressional Record,* 81st Congress, 1st Session, July 11, 1949, pp. 9205, 9208-9210.

I must vote against the pact, rather than for it . . . .

It is with great regret that I have come to my conclusion, but I have come to it because I think the pact carries with it an obligation to assist in arming, at our expense, the nations of western Europe, because with that obligation I believe it will promote war in the world rather than peace . . . . I would vote for the pact if a reservation were adopted denying any legal or moral obligation to provide arms. . . .

. . . The pact standing by itself would clearly be a deterrent to war. If Russia knows that if it starts a war it will immediately find itself at war with the United States, it is much less likely to start a war. . . . That is why I would favor the extension of the Monroe Doctrine to Europe. But if Russia sees itself ringed about gradually by so-called defensive arms, from Norway and Denmark to Turkey and Greece, it may form a different opinion. It may decide that the arming of western Europe, regardless of its present purpose, looks to an attack upon Russia. . . . They may well decide that if war is the certain result, that war might better occur now rather than after the arming of Europe is completed. . . .

The arming of western Europe cannot be achieved overnight—in fact, it will be years before the European nations could resist an all-out Russian attack. During that period, I feel that the arms policy is more likely to incite war than to deter it. . . .

. . . Let us keep our forces strong. Let us use the money we have for armament in building up the American Army, the American Air Forces, and the American Navy. Let us keep our forces strong, and spend the money that is available for arms for those forces, because in the last analysis, we will win a war only if the United States wins the war, no matter how we assist other nations. . . .

My conclusion has been reached with the greatest discomfort. . . . I would waive my other objections to the Atlantic Pact if I did not feel that it was inextricably involved with the arms program. . . . I cannot vote for a treaty which, in my opinion, will do far more to bring about a third world war than it will ever maintain the peace of the world.

# III

**SECURITY OR THREAT?**

In April 1966 French President Charles de Gaulle withdrew his nation from membership in NATO and requested the removal from French soil of United States military personnel and installations under NATO command. The following reading is excerpted from an explanation of the French position which was written in 1962 by Jean Claude Winckler, representing His Excellency Hervé Alpand, Ambassador of France to the United States. ☐ Jean Claude Winckler, "Is NATO Solid and Is It Otherwise Adequate?" Philadelphia: The Annals, Volume 342, July 1962, pp. 124-127. Copyright © 1962 by The American Academy of Political and Social Science.

I would like, at the outset, to make a very clear statement regarding France's basic position toward the alliance. I should not want to leave the slightest doubt in your mind as to where France stands. Her lot is with the free nations of the West and will remain so. . . .

Why, then, you may ask, has it been said that France wants to change the treaty? Why does she criticize NATO? Is that not weakening the pact in a time of crisis rather than strengthening it? . . .

As far as we are concerned, the pact can stand as it is; it is, rather, in the organization of it in which we think improvements could be made. . . . The founding fathers of the pact . . . knew that it would have to evolve with the times and would have to be adapted to changing circumstances. Major changes have taken place in the world since 1949: what are they?

The challenge in answer to which the treaty was signed was very specific. The idea of a regional pact came after the rape of Czechoslovakia, which brought the Western allies together. The Soviets were on the move in Europe. . . . It was to answer this direct challenge to Europe that NATO was devised, and, through it, with the full backing of the United States, Europe was saved.

NATO, however, covers one sector only: Europe and the North American continent. Since then, the Soviet challenge has become global. Korea, Indo-China, the Middle East, Africa, Cuba, Latin America were, in turn, directly or indirectly threatened. The free world must find a way to answer this global challenge. . . .

. . . [We] have asked that the Western countries having world interests—like the United States, Great Britain, and France—establish closer links of co-operation in the fields of foreign policy and global strategy.

Another change has taken place since 1949. Continental Europe at that time was still working to get back onto its feet. The ruins of the war were everywhere apparent. Europe now is again vital and prosperous. This material change is accompanied by a spiritual change. The ancient countries of Europe who had been for centuries the main actors of the international scene have found themselves with a secondary role and with a diminished voice in world affairs. . . . Their fate, they felt, was decided elsewhere, it was no longer decided in Paris, in Germany, in Rome.

This feeling, in the long run, could have brought very dangerous results. It could have created a sense of helplessness, of indifference, which, in turn, would have brought neutralism and pacifism: the "what can I do about it" attitude, the "better red than dead" slogan. People must feel, in a way, responsible for their destiny and, therefore, responsible for their defense. . . .

We feel . . . that a better balance should be found between the tasks of a unified command and governmental responsibilities. If lively interest in an Army is to be preserved, local governments, parliaments, commands must retain their shares of responsibilities in the organization of their own defense.

The other major change which has occurred since 1949 is the fact that the United States no longer possesses the monopoly of atomic weapons. . . .

It is frequently alleged that French nuclear projects were only started by General de Gaulle, that these projects reflected some sort of a personal whim of the president of the French Republic.

I wish to point out that the French nuclear program was started during the preceding regime and met with the large approval of various political parties. . . .

. . . France, and, for that matter, Europe as a whole, cannot picture itself as a reservoir of conventional forces, with nuclear forces in the hands and under the control of a non-European power. There is a very strong feeling in France about being the infantry of another country. If a partnership is to be organized between the United States and Europe, it has to be a partnership between equals, not a partnership with one part of the alliance protecting or being protected by the other part. . . .

What I wish you to remember about the French position regarding NATO is this:

(1) We want to strengthen the alliance and are prepared to make a greater financial contribution toward this aim.

(2) We will go ahead with our nuclear project even without outside help which we do not request.

(3) A French nuclear capability should result in closer ties between France, Europe, and the United States.

Under Secretary of State George Ball was interviewed in Paris on March 30, 1966 by André Fontaine of Le Monde. The following reading is excerpted from the transcript of that interview. □ "Under Secretary Ball Discusses U.S. Views on Viet-Nam and NATO." Washington, D.C.: Department of State Bulletin, Volume 54, Number 1399, April 18, 1966, p. 616.

As two Presidents of the United States have said, what we desire is a partnership between equals, from one shore of the Atlantic to the other. We have been ready for a long time to create a state of affairs in which the political decisions and responsibilities are completely shared on an equal basis, and we are anxious to attain it.

We wish to create a true association based on equality of treatment, and we have a feeling that we will not be able to obtain it fully if Europe does not take the course of unity.

We can, to be sure, practice equality of treatment in our negotiations with the European countries, but there is an aspect of equality that does not depend either on the will or the acts of the United States—namely, equality of dimensions and resources. Now, this difficulty itself would be surmounted by the establishment of a united Europe. With resources that would be very nearly the same as those of the United States, a unified Europe would be, in every respect, our equal. But this equality will never be achieved by the fragmentation of Europe, which would thus see its power and importance reduced.

The unity of Europe is, of course, an affair that concerns the Europeans and not the Americans, but we see in it the means of realizing a true association between equal countries. I wish to repeat once again that domination is the thing that is farthest from our minds. It is association that we want.

Permit me to make another point very clear. We believe in consultations, and I am always surprised to hear that we do not wish to consult anyone.

When we tried, in the past, to hold consultation in the NATO Council, the French Government now in power stated that it did not consider the Council an appropriate forum for consultations concerning the problems arising outside the area with which the treaty is concerned.

Permit me to make another remark. We regret that the French Government considered itself justified in acting unilaterally and has not presented its views on the reform of NATO to all the members of the organization, with a view to a common discussion. During the last 3 years we have repeatedly stated to the French Government that we would welcome any proposals that it might make to us. We have stated that we did not consider NATO to be a perfect or unalterable organization and that the times and conditions had changed, which fact could make changes in the form or structure of the organization necessary.

We have been told repeatedly that proposals would be communicated to us later, and we have stated very clearly that the other members of NATO and we ourselves would, together, give them most careful study. But the French Government has apparently chosen to act unilaterally.

PROBLEM 13

# Using Power
# in the Nuclear Age

The Nuclear Age was announced at Hiroshima in the last weeks of
World War II. The threat of nuclear warfare existed during the Cold
War confrontation between the Soviet Union and the United States,
whenever the latter responded to Soviet pressures with the policy of
containment. That policy raised the problem of how the United States
and the Soviet Union could each avoid direct confrontation where
nuclear force was likely to be used, and at the same time defend its
vital interests. Especially after 1949, when the Soviet Union exploded
its first atomic device, the use of force anywhere, even on a small scale,
raised the possible threat of nuclear retaliation.

During the Eisenhower administration, Secretary of State John
Foster Dulles was faced with defending American interests against
continuing Soviet pressure. He thought that almost every policy which
the United States followed after 1945 had been in response to Soviet actions and not in pursuit of long-term policy goals. Consequently, he declared the policy of "massive retaliation," which he defined as "a great
capacity to retaliate, instantly, by means and at places of our own choosing." Dulles saw nuclear weapons as one means of retaliation.

Yet the logic of "massive retaliation" soon showed its weaknesses. When Dulles' policy was originally proposed, the vast preponderance of atomic power was in American hands. As the Soviet Union piled up a huge nuclear arsenal of its own, the threat worked both ways. It was not easy, moreover, to use "massive retaliation" against subversives who operated as guerrillas.

Had "massive retaliation" been used in the Korean War, the Cuban crisis of 1962, or the Viet Nam struggle, nuclear war with its unthinkable destruction could have resulted. On each of these occasions the United States faced the problem of defending its interests without being able to use its full power. As you read, consider these questions:

1    How did MacArthur suggest that the United Nations meet the Korean aggression? How did Acheson suggest that it be handled? Why did Acheson feel that the collective security commitment in Korea demanded a different approach to Communist aggression than the one which MacArthur had suggested?

2    Why did the *Economist* praise Kennedy's diplomacy so unreservedly? On what grounds did Stone criticize that diplomacy? What evidence is there that Kennedy's position was defensible even though it threatened the use of force and possible nuclear war?

3    Compare Fulbright's and Lippmann's ideas on why the United States is involved in Viet Nam. To which man would the issue of independence in South Viet Nam be more important? Which man advocated a larger commitment for the United States? How?

4    Stone observed, "Negotiations . . . would have been better than the risk of World War III." Could negotiation actually increase the risk of World War III?

# I

## ESCALATION IN KOREA?

After the Japanese surrender in September 1945, Russian troops moved quickly through Manchuria into northern Korea. A few weeks later United States forces landed in southern Korea. The 38th parallel divided the two sections, but military commanders assumed that the United Nations would be able to reunify them. This assumption was exploded when, in June 1950, the army of North Korea, supported with Russian materials and advice, invaded South Korea. The United States immediately joined other members of the United Nations to fulfill its obligations to collective security. General Douglas

MacArthur, commander of the United Nations forces, was ready to risk all-out war. He urged bombing Communist Chinese supply bases; and, in a letter to Joseph Martin, Republican congressman from Massachusetts, he indicated his belief that Chinese troops from Taiwan should be used in Korea. The following reading is excerpted from that letter, which was written in 1951 and later made public.  □  *Congressional Record*, 82nd Congress, 1st Session, April 5, 1951, p. 3380.

My views and recommendations with respect to the situation created by Red China's entry into war against us in Korea have been submitted to Washington in most complete detail. Generally these views are well known and clearly understood, as they follow the conventional pattern of meeting force with maximum counter-force, as we have never failed to do in the past. Your view with respect to the utilization of the Chinese forces on Formosa is in conflict with neither logic nor this tradition.

It seems strangely difficult for some to realize that here in Asia is where the Communist conspirators have elected to make their play for global conquest, and that we have joined the issue thus raised on the battlefield; that here we fight Europe's war with arms while the diplomats there still fight it with words; that if we lose the war to Communism in Asia the fall of Europe is inevitable; win it, and Europe most probably would avoid war and yet preserve freedom.

As you point out, we must win. There is no substitute for victory.

On April 11, 1951, because he had challenged civilian authority, General MacArthur was relieved of his command by President Truman. On June 1 Secretary of State Dean Acheson, in hearings before the Senate Armed Services and Foreign Relations committees on the MacArthur dismissal, explained the situation facing the United States.  □  Dean Acheson, "Peace or War and the Survival of Human Freedom." Washington, D.C.: *Department of State Bulletin*, Volume 24, Number 623, June 11, 1951, pp. 923-926.

The real issues in the discussion before us are peace or war, and the survival of human freedom. It is not just a difference as to method which is now under examination. What is challenged is the bedrock purpose of our foreign policy, and of what we have been trying to do. . . .

Within the framework of the Charter of the United Nations, we have been building a collective security system based on the cooperation of those nations who are dedicated to peace. . . .

The attack on Korea . . . was a challenge to the whole system of collective security, not only in the Far East, but everywhere in the world. It was a threat to all nations newly arrived at independence. This dagger thrust pinned a warning notice to the wall which said: "Give up or be conquered."

This was a test which would decide whether our collective security system would survive or would crumble. It would determine whether other nations would be intimidated by this show of force. . . .

. . . [Our] response to the aggression against Korea required a careful estimate of the risks involved in the light of the total world situation.

There was the risk that the conflict might spread into a general war in Asia, a risk that the Chinese Communists might intervene, a risk that the Soviet Union might declare itself in.

We take it for granted that risk of some sort is implicit in any positive policy, and that there is also a risk in doing nothing. . . .

Against the dubious advantages of spreading the war in an initially limited manner to the mainland of China, there must be measured the risk of a general war with China, the risk of Soviet intervention, and of World War III, as well as the probable effects upon the solidarity of the free world coalition.

The advocates of this program make two assumptions which require careful examination. They assume that the Soviet Union will not necessarily respond to any action on our part. They also assume that in the build-up of strength relative to the Soviet Union and the Communist sphere, time is not necessarily on our side. . . .

. . . Russian self-interest in the Far East and the necessity of maintaining prestige in the Communist sphere make it difficult to see how the Soviet Union could ignore a direct attack upon the Chinese mainland. . . .

We should also analyze the effect on our allies of our taking steps to initiate the spread of war beyond Korea. It would severely weaken their ties with us and in some instances it might sever them. . . .

We cannot expect that our collective security system will long survive if we take steps which unnecessarily and dangerously expose the people who are in the system with us. They would understandably hesitate to be tied to a partner who leads them to a highly dangerous short cut across a difficult crevasse. . . .

The basic premise of our foreign policy is that time is on our side if we make good use of it. This does not necessarily mean that time must bring us to a point where we can match the Soviet Union man-for-man and tank-for-tank.

What it does mean is that we need to use the time we have to build an effective deterrent force. This requires us to create sufficient force-in-being, both in the United States and among our allies, to shield our great potential against the possibility of a quick and easy onslaught, and to ensure that our allies will not suffer occupation and destruction. And back of this shield we need to have the potential that would enable us to win a war.

# II

## MISSILES IN CUBA

In September and early October 1962, reports reached Washington that Russian missile sites were being installed in Cuba. The administration acted quickly because Russian missiles in Cuba threatened to produce future political blackmail. The following excerpt is taken from the statement which President John F. Kennedy made to the nation on October 22 explaining the situation and announcing his policy decision. On October 28 Khrushchev replied that he would remove the missiles. ☐ John F. Kennedy, "The Soviet Threat to the Americas." Washington, D.C.: *Department of State Bulletin*, Volume 47, Number 1220, November 12, 1962, pp. 715, 718.

This Government, as promised, has maintained the closest surveillance of the Soviet military buildup on the island of Cuba. Within the past week unmistakable evidence has established the fact that a series of offensive missile sites is now in preparation on that imprisoned island. The purpose of these bases can be none other than to provide a nuclear strike capability against the Western Hemisphere. . . .

The characteristics of these new missile sites indicate two distinct types of installations. Several of them include medium-range ballistic missiles capable of carrying a nuclear warhead for a distance of more than 1,000 nautical miles. Each of these missiles, in short, is capable of striking Washington, D.C., the Panama Canal, Cape Canaveral, Mexico City, or any other city in the southeastern part of the United States, in Central America, or in the Caribbean area. . . .

This urgent transformation of Cuba into an important strategic base—by the presence of these large, long-range, and clearly offensive weapons of sudden mass destruction—constitutes an explicit threat to the peace and security of all the Americas. . . .

I call upon Chairman Khrushchev to halt and eliminate this clandestine, reckless, and provocative threat to world peace and to stable relations between our two nations. I call upon him further to abandon this course of world domination and to join in an historic effort to end the perilous arms race.... He has an opportunity now to move the world back from the abyss of destruction — by returning to his Government's own words that it had no need to station missiles outside its own territory, and withdrawing these weapons from Cuba — by refraining from any action which will widen or deepen the present crisis — and then by participating in a search for peaceful and permanent solutions....

The London *Economist* promptly praised President Kennedy's action as statesmanlike and politically astute. ☐ "After Cuba." London: *The Economist*, Volume 205, Number 6219, November 3, 1962, p. 431.

Mr Kennedy, in the tense six days that began with his broadcast on October 22nd and ended last Sunday with Mr Khrushchev's promise to withdraw the offending weapons . . . from Cuba, was playing from strength.

He played his hand as a strong hand should be played: the bid called exactly, the moves unhesitating, the objective, once stated, adhered to. . . . In the last phase of the crisis the pace was becoming hot, and the hours precious: as Mr Kennedy wrote to Mr Khrushchev last Sunday when it ended, "You and I . . . were aware that developments were approaching a point where events could have become unmanageable."

Perhaps only this can explain the astonishing speed and (within the limits of the matter at issue) the completeness of the Russian retreat. Mr Kennedy thereupon showed that he knew not only how far to go, but precisely where to stop. His acceptance of Mr Khrushchev's retreat was unreserved and handsome. His conditional offers made the day before—to call off the blockade, and to give assurances against an invasion of Cuba were at once reaffirmed as "firm undertakings.". . . The Russian retreat from the western hemisphere was made as easy as it could, in the circumstances of an essentially brutal confrontation of material force, be made.

Veteran Washington correspondent I. F. Stone, in a review of the book, *The Missile Crisis* by Elie Abel, raised the question: What would have happened if Khrushchev had not backed down? ☐ I. F. Stone, "The Brink." Reprinted from *The New York Review of Books.* Copyright © 1966, The New York Review.

The essential, the terrifying, question about the missile crisis is what would have happened if Khrushchev had not backed down. . . .

The question was whether, with the whole world looking on, Kennedy would let Khrushchev get away with it. The world's first thermonuclear confrontation turned out to be a kind of ordeal by combat between two men to see which one would back down first. Schlesinger relates that in the earlier Berlin crisis, he wrote a memorandum to Kennedy protesting the tendency to define the issue as "Are you chicken or not?" But inescapably that's what the issue came around to. Schlesinger recounts an interview Kennedy gave James Wechsler of the New York *Post* in the Berlin crisis in which the President recognized that no one could win a nuclear war, that "the only alternatives were authentic negotiation or mutual annihilation," *but*—"What worried him [Kennedy] was that Khrushchev might interpret his reluctance to wage nuclear war as a symptom of an American loss of nerve . . . 'If Khrushchev wants to rub my nose in the dirt,' he told Wechsler, 'it's all over.'". . .

. . . But what if the gamble had failed? What if Khrushchev, instead of backing down when he did, had engaged in a delaying action, offering to abide by the outcome of a United Nations debate? The Republicans would have accused Kennedy of gullibility and weakness; the nuclear menace from Cuba would certainly have cost the Democrats control of the House of Representatives. After the Bay of Pigs fiasco, the damage to Kennedy's reputation might have been irreparable even if ultimately some peaceful deal to get the missiles out of Cuba were achieved. Kennedy could not wait. But the country and the world could. Negotiations, however prolonged, would have been better than the risk of World War III. This is how the survivors would have felt. Here Kennedy's political interests and the country's safety diverged. . . .

. . . Sorensen says that at one time in the inner debate Kennedy and his circle "seriously considered" either doing nothing about the missiles or limiting our response to diplomatic action only. "As some (but not all) Pentagon advisors pointed out to the President," Sorensen reveals, "we had long lived within range of Soviet missiles, we expected Khrushchev to live with our missiles nearby, and by taking this addition calmly we would prevent him from inflating its importance."

There was fear in the inner circle that our Western allies might share this cool estimate. Perhaps this was one reason we did not consult them before deciding on a showdown. . . .

Had the Cuban missile crisis erupted into a thermonuclear exchange, NATO bases in France would automatically have been involved: They would have joined in the attack and been targets for the Russians. France, like the other NATO countries, might have been destroyed without ever being consulted. It is not difficult to understand De Gaulle's distrust of an alliance in which the strongest member can plunge all the others into war without consulting them.

# III

## INVOLVEMENT IN ASIA

When the Japanese evacuated French Indo-China in 1945, the Communist Viet Minh party, led by Ho Chi Minh, tried to prevent French re-occupation of the former colony. When the French left in 1954, Viet Nam, one of the three independent nations created out of Indo-China, was divided between Communist North and Free South at the 17th parallel. Elections were scheduled for 1956, but South Viet Nam refused to permit them, arguing that the Communist North would not allow fair elections. Subsequently, the South—having involved internal difficulties—was also threatened with subversion from North Viet Nam. At the request of South Viet Nam, the United States sent military advisers. The United States then faced the problem of whether or not to commit its armed forces in South Viet Nam. The defeat of South Viet Nam by a Communist government would enhance the prestige and influence of Communist China. The fate of South Viet Nam would thus be of great consequence to other nations in Southeast Asia. Democrat J. William Fulbright of Arkansas, chairman of the Senate Foreign Relations Committee, discussed the problem in 1964. ☐ Condensed from *Old Myths and New Realities*, by J. W. Fulbright. Copyright © 1964 by J. William Fulbright. Reprinted by permission of Random House, Inc. and Jonathan Cape Limited.

The situation in Vietnam poses a... need for a re-evaluation of American policy. Other than withdrawal, which I do not think can be realistically considered under present circumstances, there are three options open to us in Vietnam: first, the continuation of the anti-guerrilla war within South Vietnam, along with renewed American efforts to increase the military effectiveness of the South Vietnamese Army and the political effectiveness of the South Vietnamese Government; second, an attempt to end the war through negotiations for the neutralization of South Vietnam or of both North and South Vietnam; and finally, the expansion of the scale of the war, either by the direct commitment of American forces or by equipping the South Vietnamese armed forces to attack North Vietnamese territory, possibly by means of commando-type operations from the sea or air.

It is difficult to see how a negotiation, under present military circumstances, could lead to the termination of the war under conditions that would preserve the freedom of South Vietnam. It is extremely difficult for a party to a negotiation to achieve by diplomacy objectives which it has conspicuously failed to win by warfare. The hard fact of the matter is that our bargaining position is at present a weak one, and until the equation of advantages between the two sides has been substantially altered in our favor, there can be little prospect of a negotiated settlement which would secure the independence of a non-Communist South Vietnam. . . .

It seems clear that there are only two realistic options open to us in Vietnam in the immediate future: the expansion of the conflict in one way or another, or a renewed effort to bolster the capacity of the South Vietnamese to prosecute the war successfully on its scale. . . . It should be clear to all concerned that the United States will continue to defend its vital interests with respect to Vietnam.

Our purpose is . . . to establish viable, independent states in Indochina and elsewhere in Southeast Asia, which will be free of and secure from the domination of Communist China and Communist North Vietnam. I emphasize that we wish these nations to be *free of and secure from* domination by Peking and Hanoi, but not necessarily hostile to these regimes. Our objective is not . . . to establish our own military power in Indochina or in any way to bring the nations of the Indochinese peninsula under our own domination or even to bring them into an American "sphere of influence."

These, I believe, are some, although by no means all, of the issues of foreign policy in which it is essential to re-evaluate long-standing ideas and commitments in the light of new and changing realities.

Walter Lippmann, a noted political commentator for half a century, argued in 1964 that a military solution to the Viet Nam crisis was not possible. □ Walter Lippmann, "Our Problem in Viet Nam." Copyright, Newsweek, Inc. September, 1964.

Our situation in South Vietnam is almost exactly that of man who, when a bear came at him, grabbed it by the tail. His problem then was how to get rid of the bear if he let go of its tail. . . . [Our] problem in Southeast Asia is how we can induce the Communist bear (North Vietnam backed by Red China) to leave the whole of Indochina alone . . . .

The problem is hard to solve. For the Communists think they are winning the war. They think that South Vietnam is breaking up in the disorders of the Buddhists and the Catholics and of the ambitious generals and the politicians. The Communists believe that victory is in sight, a victory in which they will engineer the downfall of the Saigon government and its replacement by one which will ask the Americans to leave the country. . . .

. . . It seems so simple to argue that the war in Vietnam can be won if we knock out North Vietnam which is supporting the war. But in fact it is not simple at all to win the war by bombing North Vietnam. The Hanoi infantry and behind it the inexhaustible infantry of China can overrun South Vietnam and Laos and Cambodia without meeting any serious resistance from the demoralized and war-weary troops that Saigon commands.

Thus, we find that a military solution cannot be had by aiding and supporting the South Vietnamese alone; it cannot be had by attacking North Vietnam. How are we to bring about a negotiated settlement which is not a surrender, which does not yield Indochina to conquest by Red China, and which is respectable in that the feeble little nations of what used to be called Indochina have a reasonable chance to govern themselves?

It is easier to ask that question than it is to answer it, and I have no magic formula to offer. But there may be, in fact I think there are, certain strategic principles which can be applied to the problem. The first is the old American military doctrine, which was first breached in the Korean War, that the vital interests of the United States cannot be defended by becoming involved in a land war on the continent of Asia. . . . It is with a lingering respect for this old established American strategic principle that our government refuses to call what is going on in South Vietnam a "war." . . .

The second strategic principle is that at sea and in the air American military power is paramount in the whole Pacific and capable of being paramount in the Indian Ocean as well. This means that if eventually we come to an agreement which involves withdrawal of American troops from Saigon, we shall still have very great power and influence in the Far East. The notion propagated by some, that we are in danger of being driven back to Hawaii or Seattle, is nonsense.

The hope of bringing about an acceptable negotiated settlement lies in the fact that no matter what happens in the jungles of Indochina, Hanoi and Peking can never be at peace, can never be secure, unless they come to terms with the sea and air power of the United States.

The existence of this enormous power will someday permit us to hold back the Communist bear and to let go of his tail.

PROBLEM 14

# Diplomatic Recognition
# and Communist China

In late 1949 Communist armies took full control of mainland China and sent the Nationalist government of Chiang Kai-shek fleeing to the island of Taiwan (Formosa). With the establishment of two Chinese governments, one on the mainland controlling 600 million people and the other on Taiwan controlling 11 million people, a problem of recognition faced United States policy makers. Should the United States give diplomatic recognition to Communist China or should it support Chiang's Nationalists, World War II allies of the United States?

Obtaining the recognition of other countries confers prestige on a nation. A revolutionary government needs to be acknowledged as the legal government to clear the way for political and commercial agreements with other nations.

On what basis do nations generally recognize one another? One test frequently applied to a new regime asks: does it have the power to control its people, to defend its boundaries, and to fulfill its obligations to other nations? If a revolutionary regime does have that power, regardless of how it achieved it, other nations consider that regime to be the *de facto* government (the government in fact), with whom diplomatic relations should be conducted. Throughout the history of the United States, policy makers have followed this standard. Thomas Jefferson expressed his faith in it when he said: "We surely cannot deny to any Nation that right whereon our own government is founded, that everyone may govern itself according to whatever form it pleases, and change these forms at will."

Other considerations have influenced the decision of the United States to refuse recognition to Communist China. Especially in the twentieth century, disapproval of a regime on moral grounds has kept the United States from recognizing some new governments. One example is Woodrow Wilson's dislike of the Huerta dictatorship in Mexico in 1913. The moral consideration is evident regarding Communist China. Does it *deserve* to be recognized? Is the United States committed to continued recognition of the Taiwan regime as official China because of earlier promises to Chiang Kai-shek?

The anticipation of political or economic consequences speeds or delays recognition. Doubtful at first that the Communist regime would survive in China, Western nations were reluctant to recognize it. However, the doubts of the 1950's virtually disappeared by the 1960's and a number of nations have recognized Communist China. If the United States continues to refuse recognition, how might other nations regard the United States? The problem of recognition is complicated by the fact that in 1945 Nationalist China under Chiang became one of the five permanent members of the Security Council of the United Nations, and has remained a member since. American recognition of Communist China would certainly weaken the position of Nationalist China in the United Nations. Could continued exclusion of China from the United Nations encourage it to become more aggressive in Southeast Asia? On the other hand, would recognition give Communist China added prestige, endorse its aggressive policy, or demoralize the Asian allies of the United States?

Another reason for American non-recognition is Communist antagonism, demonstrated by open support of North Korea in the Korean War of 1950-1953 and of the Viet Cong in the Viet Nam war of the 1960's.

Despite the existence of old sympathies and new antagonisms, some Americans have argued that the policy of non-recognition is unrealistic and ineffective, and that a careful reassessment of policy is necessary. The readings which follow present varying points of view on the issue. As you read, consider these questions:

1    What criteria for the recognition of a nation were used in the case of Communist China, according to Dulles? What does he mean by "recognition is always a privilege, not a right"?

2    Why does Younger think that the United States should recognize Communist China? Why does Feis think that the United States should not recognize Communist China? Which argument, do you think, is more reasonable? Why?

3    What does Elegant mean by saying that American policy toward Communist China is not a "reasoned" one? If China refused to accept recognition on terms offered by the United States, what would be the implications to American policy?

4    What are the "old myths and new realities" which Fulbright refers to? What are the "unthinkable things" he is urging Americans to think?

# I

## RECOGNITION AS A POLITICAL MOVE

John Foster Dulles, Secretary of State in the Eisenhower administration, described the criteria used by the United States in deciding against the recognition of Communist China.   ☐ John Foster Dulles, "Our Policies Toward Communism in China." Washington, D.C.: *Department of State Bulletin*, Volume 37, Number 942, July 15, 1957, pp. 92-94.

If we seemed to waver and to compromise with communism in China, that would in turn weaken free Asia resistance to the Chinese Communist regime and assist international communism to score a great success in its program to encircle us.

United States recognition of Communist China would make it probable that the Communist regime would obtain the seat of China in the United Nations. That would not be in the interest either of the United States or of the United Nations.

The United Nations is not a reformatory for bad governments. It is supposedly an association of those who are already "peace-loving" and who are "able and willing to carry out" the charter obligations. The basic obligation is not to use force, except in defense against armed attack.

The Chinese Communist regime has a record of successive armed aggressions, including war against the United Nations itself, a war not

144

yet politically settled but discontinued by an armistice. The regime asserts not only its right but its purpose to use force if need be to bring Taiwan under its rule. . . .

There are some who say that we should accord diplomatic recognition to the Communist regime because it has now been in power so long that it has won the *right* to that.

That is not sound international law. Diplomatic recognition is always a privilege, never a right.

Of course, the United States knows that the Chinese Communist regime exists. We know that very well, for it has fought us in Korea. . . .

But diplomatic recognition gives the recognized regime valuable rights and privileges, and, in the world of today, recognition by the United States gives the recipient much added prestige and influence at home and abroad. . . .

Other customary tests are whether, as Thomas Jefferson put it, the recognized government reflects "the will of the nation, substantially declared"; whether the government conforms to the code of civilized nations, lives peacefully, and honors its international obligations.

Always, however, recognition is admitted to be an instrument of national policy, to serve enlightened self-interest.

One thing is established beyond a doubt. There is nothing automatic about recognition. It is never compelled by the mere lapse of time.

# II

### IS AMERICAN POLICY IMPRACTICAL?

Kenneth Younger, a Labour party member of the British House of Commons, believed that the alternative to recognizing Communist China was war. He questioned the premises and practicality of American policy toward Communist China. ☐ Kenneth Younger, "Critique of American China Policy." *Western World*, September 1957, pp. 30-34. Reprinted by permission of the author.

The controversy over policy towards . . . China has centered around three main questions. Should the People's Government in Peking be diplomatically recognized? Should it occupy the Chinese seat in the United Nations? And what should be the trading and cultural relations between Communist China and the Western World? . . .

. . . United States government spokesmen have justified their policy in terms appropriate to a state of war. Communist China, they say, is bent on world domination. It is an aggressor and morally and politically unfit to be a member of the United Nations. There is no point, they assert, in having cultural relations, let ... [alone] diplomatic ones, with such a pariah while any form of trade with it can only have the effect of strengthening a government which must be regarded as an enemy. . . .

Dulles has recently replied to the obvious query as to why the United States does not treat the Soviet Union as it treats China, by saying that the United States would not have recognized the Soviet government in 1933 if it had then known how the Soviet Union would subsequently behave. Does anyone, however, really think that if the United States had refused all contact with the Soviet Union over the years, this would have advanced the cause of peace? . . .

Closely linked with diplomatic recognition is the question of China's representation in the United Nations. China is, under the Charter, a member of the organization and a permanent member of the Security Council. The United States, when asked why, in these circumstances, it will not contemplate China being represented in the United Nations by the government which has controlled China for eight years, gives two replies. The first, heard more faintly every year, is that the Peking government's grip on China may be broken at any minute. No one, however, believes this. It is strictly for the record. The second reply is that the Chinese government's behavior unfits it for membership in the world club. . . .

. . . If the United Nations is to do its job of settling disputes without war, those governments, wicked or virtuous, which are at loggerheads, must be able to meet there. The more they disapprove of each other, the more important it is that their confrontation should take place within the organization. . . .

Quite as important is the effect of United States policies upon the rest of Asia. . . . For Asian countries, it is self-evident that they must seek co-existence with the communist regime in China. China to them looms larger than Russia and seems a much more permanent factor in the Asian scene than the United States. They do not believe that Chiang Kai-shek's government will ever see China again, nor do they expect the collapse of the mainland regime. . . .

From the point of view of mutual confidence within the Western alliance, there is one further urgent need. It is to demonstrate that the United States is now framing its policies in the Far East, as it is already doing in other areas, upon the basis of an honest appraisal of world events and not upon the basis of prejudices deriving from its own domestic situation and its isolationist past.

... When the moment of decision arrives, it is the realities which are added up and form the basis of action, but the resulting disillusionment can do a lot of damage. Worst of all, prolonged dissemination of romantic myths ends by creating a public opinion, rooted in unreality, which itself becomes a stubborn obstacle to statesmanship.

# III

## "UNLESS WE ARE REASONABLY ASSURED"

Herbert Feis, an American historian and a student of Chinese affairs, explained his belief that recognition is not desirable until Communist China changes its attitudes toward the United States and modifies its aggressive policies. □ Herbert Feis, "The United States and China." Cambridge, Massachusetts: *Daedalus*, Volume 91, Number 4, Fall 1962, pp. 792, 795-796, 799. Copyright © 1962 by the American Academy of Arts and Sciences.

[The] Chinese Communist view of society predisposes Mao Tse-tung and his colleagues to believe that the United States will never cease to try to destroy Communism in China, and this discredits the possibility of living in peaceful "coexistence" with us. In their eyes, our determined protection of Chiang Kai-shek confirms that opinion. . . . For in their book, Communist use of force to subdue other peoples is only the necessary and justified prelude to "liberation" of their victims. . . .

The most commonly heard reasons for the policy which may be called "unreserved initiative for recognition," are impressive. Thus the two connected suppositions on which it rests ought to be explicitly stated and examined.

One is that the hostility and aggression of the Chinese Communist government is due primarily to our past and present treatment of it. . . . The historical experience does not support the view that the current Chinese Communist attitude is due primarily to mistreatment by others or is sufficiently explained by past grievances. . . .

The second supposition is that, in this situation as in most others, the best, perhaps the only, way to win friendship and trust is to show friendship and trust. Perhaps so. But I think it more likely that the Chinese Communist rulers at present really do not care a whit for the friendship, esteem or trust of the Western capitalist democracies, though they may purposely pretend to do so now and then. They would probably construe recognition and admission into the United Nations, not as a gesture of friendly acceptance, but as an act of contrition, a diplomatic expedient, and a tribute to the strength of Communist influence. Nor would they be wholly wrong in these inferences. . . .

But we should maintain our refusal of recognition and our resistance to the admission of Communist China to the United Nations, until and unless we are reasonably assured that the regime will not use force against Taiwan, strive and conspire to bring about a Communist revolution in Japan, and cease to challenge the conception of peaceful coexistence. If the Chinese Communist government would give reliable indications that it will so curb its actions and amend its attitudes, then the American government should venture to recognize it and enter into a truce of toleration with it. . . .

Whether or not we recognize Communist China, we are in for an unpleasant time. We must maintain a military force so formidable that our diplomacy need not yield to fear or threats. Yet we must be sure that our diplomacy does not reject any fair chance to settle our quarrels with Communist China or the Soviet Union on terms that provide both ourselves and them freedom from fear.

# IV

## DOES CHINA WANT RECOGNITION?

Robert Elegant served as Southeast Asia correspondent for *Newsweek* from 1956 to 1962. Believing that the United States must accept the existence of Communist China, Elegant warned in *The Center of the World* that the road to recognition might be a difficult one. □ From *The Center of the World* by Robert S. Elegant. Copyright © 1963, 1964 by Robert S. Elegant. Reprinted by permission of Doubleday & Company, Inc. and Methuen & Company, Ltd.

Despite her domestic difficulties, China is a major force in the great world. Still inclined to consider her a curious natural phenomenon rather than a nation, the foreign powers can no longer discount China's influence. Peking is actively involved not only with the life of the Communist bloc and with events on her own borders, but also with disarmament negotiations and the tides of world trade. The vexing question of China affects Washington's relations with all its allies—and the uncommitted nations. American energies are once more deeply committed to a war against Communist expansion, this time in Vietnam, where the Chinese stand sponsor. . . .

... [The] Communist government is firmly in control of China and likely to retain that control indefinitely. Despite the periodic relaxation of pressure dictated by their doctrines as well as their difficulties, the Communist leaders have not materially altered either their goals or the manner in which they plan to attain those goals. . . .

Present American policy toward Communist China resists logical analysis because it is not a reasoned growth, but the sum total of a series of improvisations, emotional reactions, and responses to internal political pressures. The attempt to isolate China, economically and politically, does, however, appear to be based upon the implicit assumption that the Communist regime will not endure. American actions are presumably designed to hasten its passing. But the People's Republic has, despite its difficulties, consolidated its internal position and increased its external power in the fourteen years that have passed since its establishment and the nearly simultaneous adoption of the present American attitude. . . .

It is exceedingly difficult for the United States to formulate and carry out a reasoned policy toward China. Just as China feels herself misused by the West, the United States feels that China under the Communists is repaying a century of devoted friendship with abuse and threats. Both attitudes have a basis in reality, and both also rest upon a large measure of self-deception. But those antagonistic Chinese and American attitudes have themselves become realities in the sense that they determine the actions of two governments. . . . Since China policy must, of necessity, be the heart of any effective Asian policy, the American commitment to an illogical hope that the Peking regime will, somehow, vanish is detrimental to our interests . . . throughout Asia. . . .

The Communists would undoubtedly refuse the offer of recognition, unless it was accompanied by cession of Formosa. That concession is unthinkable. Even rejected, a sincere offer of recognition would free American policy of many of the burdens it carries in Asia today. The United States operates under a considerable diplomatic disadvantage because much of Asia feels that Washington, vengefully and unreasonably, is setting its face against reality by refusing to recognize Communist China and permit her admission to the United Nations. Peking successfully plays the martyr, although she does not really want American recognition and certainly does not want it without Formosa. An offer to recognize Communist sovereignty over the area Peking actually does rule would deprive the Communists of their most reliable enemy and would shift the onus on nonrecognition to China. She would change roles, herself appearing unreasonable, while the United States became the obvious victim of Peking's irrationality and stubbornness. Recognition would also allay lingering fears in Asia that the United States seeks to restore a vanished *status quo* for economic reasons. Finally, the Communists in time might well come to the realization that normalizing trade relations with the United States would be to their own advantage. That recognition could be the beginning of a new adjustment to reality. In the meantime, increasing trade between Western Europe and Communist China, which the United States cannot halt even if it should want to, is a desirable means of keeping open the channels of communication between Peking and the outside world—as well as demonstrating to Peking that alternative sources are available to replace dwindling Soviet trade.

# V

## "THINK THE UNTHINKABLE"

Democratic Senator J. William Fulbright of Arkansas, chairman of the Senate Foreign Relations Committee and an occasional critic of the foreign policies of the Johnson administration, warned against "old myths" in dealing with Communist China.   □ *The New York Times*, March 26, 1964, p. 12. Copyright © 1964 by The New York Times Company. Reprinted by permission.

The Far East is another area of the world in which American policy is handicapped by the divergence of the old myths and the new realities. ... We are committed, with respect to China and other areas in Asia, to inflexible policies of long standing from which we hesitate to depart because of the attribution to these policies of an aura of mystical sanctity.

I do not think that the United States can or should recognize Communist China or acquiesce in its admission to the United Nations under present circumstances. It would be unwise to do so because there is nothing to be gained by it so long as the Peking regime maintains its attitude of implacable hostility toward the United States. I do not believe, however, that this state of affairs is necessarily permanent. ...

We would do well ... to maintain an "open door" to the possibility of improved relations with Communist China in the future. For a start we must jar open our minds to certain realities about China, of which the foremost is that there are not really "two Chinas" but only one, mainland China, and that it is ruled by Communists and likely to remain so for the indefinite future.

Once we accept this fact, it becomes possible to reflect on the conditions under which it might be possible for us to enter into relatively normal relations with mainland China. One condition, of course, must be the abandonment by the Communist Chinese, tacitly if not explicitly, of their intention to conquer and incorporate Taiwan. This seems unlikely now, but far more surprising changes have occurred in politics, and it is possible that a new generation of leaders in Peking and Taipei may put a quiet end to the Chinese civil war, opening the possibility of entirely new patterns of international relations in the Far East.

Should such changes occur, they will open up important opportunities for American policy, and it is to be hoped that we will be able and willing to take advantage of them. It seems possible, for example, that an atmosphere of reduced tension in the Far East might make it possible to strengthen world peace by drawing mainland China into existing East-West agreements in such fields as disarmament, trade and educational exchange. . . .

. . . American policy has to one degree or another been less effective than it might have been because of our national tendency to equate means with ends and therefore to attach a mythological sanctity to policies and practices which in themselves have no moral content or value except insofar as they contribute to the achievement of some valid national objective.

I believe that we must try to overcome this excessive moralism, which binds us to old myths and, worse still, leads us to regard new and unfamiliar ideas with fear and mistrust.

We must dare to think about "unthinkable" things. We must learn to explore all of the options and possibilities that confront us in a complex and rapidly changing world. . . .

A creative foreign policy—as President Truman, for one, knew—is not necessarily one which wins immediate approval. It is sometimes necessary for leaders to do unpleasant and unpopular things . . . . We must dare to think about "unthinkable things," because when things become "unthinkable," thinking stops and action becomes mindless.

# The Complexities
# of Policy Making

Foreign policy is far more complicated today than it was only a generation ago. Diplomats and policy makers are not only obliged to consider and assess new issues but are also frequently forced to act quickly as incidents demand immediate attention. Critics condemned the United States for precipitous action in Cuba in 1962. But in some situations policy makers have believed that tardy action could have had serious consequences. When China attacked the northern frontier of India in 1962, a part of the Free World was challenged by Communism; and policy makers considered several questions: Is the incident a "local issue" or is it a threat to the Free World? Would sending troops or other aid deter the Chinese or would it provoke further aggression?

Two factors that obviously complicate policy making are the persistent efforts of the Soviet Union to extend its political doctrine and the proliferation of nuclear weapons. Not so obvious, but of increasing significance, is another factor which has developed since World War II. It is the expansion of the United Nations from its original fifty nations to one hundred seventeen in January 1966. During the early years of that organization, the United States could exercise greater influence in the deliberations and actions of the United Nations than it can today. The newly emergent Afro-Asian nations play a role of increasing importance in the United Nations. For instance, the United States has successfully prevented the admission of Communist China to the United Nations. But the smaller nations, each with an equal vote, may decide that recognition must be accorded Communist China. The United Nations will undoubtedly play an increasingly important role in international affairs, and consequently the United States will be obliged to conduct its foreign policy with more concern for the opinions of United Nations members.

The emergence of many new nations since the mid-1950's has seriously complicated international relations. Disorder in the Congo, internal conflict in Indonesia, and military coups d'état in Ghana and Nigeria were more than local disturbances. Each had world-wide repercussions. These and other complicating factors are discussed in the following readings. As you read, consider these questions:

1    How did the Rockefeller Report reconcile the basic American objective of survival and the grand objective of peace? How did Jackson reconcile these two objectives? Did Rusk express a broader objective than that discussed in the Rockefeller Report? How?

2    How are present American foreign policy objectives different from or similar to goals of the early post-war period?

3    Why did Aron criticize American concern for the opinions of Afro-Asian nations? Rusk believed that the policy maker must consider the building of a decent world order. Spanier believed that the United States must be its "brother's keeper." How might Aron have agreed or disagreed with these two positions?

4    What, in your opinion, would be a good American policy toward uncommitted nations?

# I

## AMERICAN OBJECTIVES

*The Mid-Century Challenge to U.S. Foreign Policy,* presenting the views of a panel of experts in foreign relations, is a report of the Rockefeller Brothers Fund Special Studies Project.  ☐ From *The Mid-Century Challenge to U.S. Foreign Policy.* Copyright © 1959 by Rockefeller Brothers Fund, Inc. (As it appears in *Prospect for America,* © 1961). Reprinted by permission of Doubleday & Company, Inc.

The United States as it moves down the second half of the twentieth century finds itself in a world of great dangers and great opportunities. Through actions and choices in the field of foreign policy, the United States must come to terms with this world. It must show how it means to use the power which has been bestowed upon it, and how it can best live up to responsibilities which . . . have been thrust upon it. . . .

. . . The present generation must establish a sane but imaginative concept of what foreign policy can accomplish and then go on and do the work which it will require. . . .

What are the objectives of American policy? . . .

That it is not the objective of the United States to extend its territorial dominion may seem obvious to Americans. But in fact the opposite has been the rule through much of our own history and for most nations. The United States has provided an example of territorial expansion—by settlement, by purchase, by war. By the beginning of the twentieth century the present boundaries of the U.S. had been filled out and the transient dream of further empire once and for all renounced. That no territorial ambitions or desires now stir America, that there is not even debate on this point, needs to be stressed. . . .

It needs next to be said that the American objective includes the basic, fundamental one of national survival.

A nation, like an individual, need perhaps give no reason for wanting to survive. A deep instinct and an unreasoning will are, in the last analysis, what count. But the age in which we live justifies making this objective explicit and affirming it solemnly. The threat to the survival of the United States is today greater than this country has ever experienced, even in its first uncertain years as a nation. It is confronted by a hostile power system equipped with weapons of destruction which pose for the rest of the world the issue of survival in its starkest form. . . .

Putting the issue in terms of survival confronts foreign policy with its grimmest decision: the resort to force and the possible use of weapons dangerous to civilization itself. It confronts the citizens and their leaders with the ultimate question: upon what grounds do they deem their survival as a nation a good for the sake of which such grave perils must be faced? For Americans, the answer must be that, despite shortcomings and defects, they conceive the United States as standing for enduring values deeply rooted in the aspirations of man. Nothing less than that conviction can sustain them against the final test.

Peace is obviously one of the grand objectives of American foreign policy. The American people do not like war, have never liked it, and find their attitude powerfully reinforced by the form which future wars must take. The only question is whether peace shall be the whole aim of foreign policy; whether everything shall be yielded to that end. Clearly the answer must be *no*. The risks which arise from the possibility of war are great. But by resolutely accepting the risk—and by that alone— we gain a decent chance of avoiding it. . . .

. . . Peace is not a single or simple thing. It can only be the result of a nation's total policies, within the total policies of all the other nations. It is the end product of a wide series of arrangements, institutions, habits and organizations, all in working order. A foreign policy which devoted itself exclusively to avoiding war would neglect the constructive aspects out of which a true peace must develop. A free nation which sought nothing but peace would gain peace only at the price of its freedom.

In this area, as in that of national survival, we meet a paradox. The nation, regardless of risks, must preserve itself, just at a point where the significance of the nation-state is declining. So the possibility of war must be faced even though it is difficult to conceive of war as a suitable instrument of policy.

Secretary of State Dean Rusk spoke before the American Political Science Association at Washington, D.C. in September 1965. In discussing how foreign policy decisions are made, he pointed out the objectives which guide policy makers. ☐ Dean Rusk, "The Anatomy of Foreign Policy Decisions." Washington, D.C.: *Department of State Bulletin,* Volume 53, Number 1370, September 27, 1965, pp. 502-505, 508.

I wish . . . to talk about a professional concern which you and we in government share: the anatomy of foreign policy decisions. . . .

What questions should a foreign policy officer ask himself before he takes off on a policy? How does he avoid the fatal flaw which comes from overlooking a factor which proves to be decisive in the flow of events? Let me emphasize that I am not now talking about bureaucratic procedure . . . but about the thought processes of those who are involved in a decision . . . .

The first requirement is to identify accurately the question which has to be answered. In many situations the very framing of the question strongly affects the answer. . . .

Once we are satisfied that we have honestly and accurately posed the question, the policy officer must try to insure his command of the factual situation. Does he have all of the facts relevant to the answer?

Is there further information that he must get? Which are the crucial facts? Has he pulled them out of the heap of jackstraws adequately? Has he separated hard fact from speculation and estimate? Is he aware of the gradations of reliability among his facts?

Policy operates on the future—and the future cannot be surely known. But a solid grasp of fact—and how elusive this is—is essential to a relevant judgment.

Having the question and the relevant facts before us, we then ask, which U.S. interests, objectives, or responsibilities are involved? To put it more baldly, what difference does it make to us?

To answer this, we have first to look at the immediate political, economic, and security interests of the United States. We need to know which of these interests are involved in the problem at hand and how they would be affected by the alternative answers.

But we have to examine a larger question: How will the outcome of this problem affect the building of a decent world order—the kind of world envisaged in the U.N. Charter?

We ask this question . . . because the largest American interests are directly involved in its realization. Four postwar American administrations have recognized that these interests could not be protected merely by meeting immediate threats as they arose. We have not only to put out fires, as they break out, but also to try to build a more fireproof structure—a more secure world. . . .

In a sense this effort can be compared to the building of a house. A large number of individual bricks must be put together in ways that add up to the desired result. Many of the specific foreign problems that we face seem small and unexciting. But how they fall into place will help to decide whether the house goes up. The wise policymaker will also see what past American policies or commitments are involved. . . .

This is not to say that past commitments should never be changed. But the policymaker should be aware of the costs of changing them before deciding whether to set them aside.

He should also look to the future commitments involved in the course that he is proposing. What shadow will this course cast over later policymakers?

Few foreign problems can be solved by the United States alone. In facing most problems, therefore, the policymaker must assess what other governments will think about it. Who are the other interested parties? This means not only who claims to have an interest but how much and what kind of interest. . . .

The founders of this country, in declaring its independence, spoke of their "decent respect to the opinions of mankind." And so it is today. While the views of bystanders should not act as a bar to needed action, we want to take account of them, in shaping or explaining our action, as, indeed, we want to know the views of those who would make themselves our adversaries.

We want the emerging world order to be one which can eventually encompass every country—to be one in which each country can freely manage its own affairs. We are not trying to build a community which excludes anyone or is directed against anyone. . . .

. . . Steadily the policy officer works his way through the alternative answers—testing, rejecting, or revising them. In most matters he will find none which is completely satisfactory. He does not live in Utopia but in a real world filled with human frailty—including his own. He cannot find logical and consistent answers for situations filled with contradictions. He is the first to know that his answer is subject to criticism from one flank or the other. But he cannot avoid an answer. For inaction is itself a policy decision.

Senator Henry M. Jackson, Democrat from Washington, discussed common assumptions about foreign policy at a lecture at Boston College in May 1965. The following reading is excerpted from that lecture. □ Henry M. Jackson, "Facts, Fallacies and Foreign Policy." New York: Vital Speeches of the Day. Volume 31, Number 17, June 15, 1965, pp. 516-518.

In recent months, the college campus has become a forum—and in the case of some groups a target—for the advocacy of ill-conceived and false notions of foreign and defense policy. In many cases demonstrations—some of them disorderly—have been a substitute for what should be an informed and orderly debate.

Let me discuss with you certain mistaken assumptions about international affairs that crop up repeatedly.

. . . One false notion is that communism is a unified force—a really monolithic international movement.

There was a time, in the years following World War II and ending roughly with the death of Stalin in 1953, when communism appeared to be a unified force, centrally directed from the Kremlin. . . .

Today the contest for leadership of world communism is as bitter as only family quarrels can be. But the family, however deeply split, is still a family. Were Peking's hold on power to be seriously threatened from within or without, Moscow might and probably would come to Peking's aid. And vice versa—even though that may be difficult to imagine today.

In short, the real world is gray, not black and white. Communism is not a monolithic force: even a junior grade satellite like Cuba does not dance always to the Soviet tune. But neither does the split go so deep that the family could not patch up its quarrels long enough to aid a member whose survival was in jeopardy. . . .

. . . *A more and more common fallacy, as a generation comes to maturity that did not experience the 30's and 40's first-hand, is that preparedness is the road to war and disarmament is the road to peace.* . . .

It is not a pleasant fact to recall but the truth is that the peace movement of the 30's helped to bring on World War II, not to prevent it. . . .

The true champions of peace today, as in the 30's, are those who understand that power must be used, with restraint but also with assurance, to keep the peace, or to restore it. . . .

. . . *Another frequent error is that "America can do anything" and that American power can always succeed if we will only use it.* . . .

. . . [Power] is relative. It cannot be measured except in relation to another's power. Strictly speaking, it makes no sense to say, as we often do, that the United States is strong. We should use the comparative —the United States is stronger—or weaker—in this or that respect than some other state.

Power is the ability to produce intended effects. Power is, in other words, the ability to bend others to one's will. Even military force is, in the final analysis, a tool of persuasion. In Korea we sought to persuade the Chinese to accept the unification of Korea on our terms. They were not persuaded. In turn, they sought to persuade us to accept unification on their terms. We were not persuaded. In the final outcome, each side was persuaded to accept roughly the *status quo ante* because the price of accomplishing unification on its terms proved to be too high.

Thus, power is relative in a second sense: it is not only relative to the power of adversaries but it is relative to the goals sought. The more limited one's objectives the more limited is the power that has to be brought to bear in achieving them. This point has relevance today in Vietnam. . . .

. . . *Another familiar illusion . . . is that negotiation around a conference table is an alternative to the risks and burdens of the cold war.* . . .

158

Negotiation is not a substitute for pressure. Pressure is a part of the negotiating process. It is an old rule that a diplomat cannot be expected to win more at the bargaining table than his comrade-in-arms has won—or is clearly in a position to win—on the field of battle. . . .

A good many Americans still have to learn the lesson. Negotiation is not talk apart from action—negotiation is talk *and* action. Indeed, the outcome of discussions *inside* the conference room is likely to be decided by the whole series of pressures *outside* the conference room. All these pressures, including military moves, determine whether an international discussion can be brought to a satisfactory end. . . .

History does not award its prizes in terms of the merits of one's cause—but in terms of the efficacy of one's efforts on behalf of his cause.

# II

## AMERICA AND WORLD-WIDE PERSPECTIVE

Professor Raymond Aron, a political commentator in France, puts American policy into perspective with relation to the newly emergent nations of Africa and Asia. □ Raymond Aron, "Reflections on American Diplomacy." Cambridge, Massachusetts: Daedalus, Volume 91, Number 4, Fall 1962, pp. 717, 721-722. Copyright © 1962 by the American Academy of Arts and Sciences.

Let us start with a proposition that is obvious but often overlooked: the United States has and must have a world-wide diplomacy, whereas European nations, even Great Britain and France, no longer have the resources required for action on a world scale. . . .

This difference between a world-wide perspective and a purely European one has been responsible for misunderstandings and tensions between the United States and its European allies. . . . The European realist does not at all dispute the idea that the United States should keep in touch with the Afro-Asian nations as much as possible and influence them away from the Soviet bloc. What he questions is the conception of competing for the allegiance of the uncommitted nations formulated by the American diplomat, and the methods he uses to win out over his rival.

Is it wise to give representatives of the new nations an exaggerated idea of their own importance? Is it right to let them believe that their words or commitments will seriously affect the relationships of world power? Is it advisable to flatter them and suggest that we need them, when they in fact need us much more? . . . To the European realist, nothing seems more ridiculous than the attention paid by the State Department or the White House to what they call "world opinion."

There is no such thing as world opinion on the political level. The representatives of the uncommitted nations meeting in Belgrade did not condemn the Soviet resumption of nuclear tests, but they would have denounced the United States indignantly if it had taken the same initiative. Why this double standard, to use an American expression? . . . [The] uncommitted nations are more afraid of the U.S.S.R. than of the United States, they know the Soviets are less sensitive to moral condemnation, they are naturally more anti-capitalist than anti-Communist. They know that positive neutralism—that is, noncommitment expressed in language closer to the language of the Soviets than to that of the West, in general pays off. Positive neutralism, shrewdly practiced, often leads to competitive bidding among the great powers for the good will of the neutrals, even to competitive financial generosity. The lesson is simple: the uncommitted nations are not the arbiters of justice and injustice; popular opinion and the opinion of politicians is no more impartial in the neutral world than in the West or in the Soviet bloc.

Historian John Spanier advocated heavy economic aid to the new nations by the United States. ☐ John W. Spanier, *American Foreign Policy Since World War II*, pp. 187, 189-192. 2nd edn. New York: Frederick A. Praeger, Inc., copyright © 1962. London: Pall Mall Press, 1962.

Any American policy toward the underdeveloped areas must start with the recognition that the future of these countries will play an important role in the survival of the United States. America cannot allow the gulf between the rich and poor nations to widen—for the same reason that this gap could not be allowed to exist *within* each of the Western nations 100 years ago. The two situations are, in fact, so amazingly similar that the lessons of the previous experience can easily be applied to the present international division of wealth. As the Industrial Revolution gathered momentum in each of the European countries and America, it created a privileged minority which owned most of the wealth. The distribution of income was, to say the least, unequal. . . .

It is this same problem of an inequitable distribution of income which once again plagues the world. Only this time the problem does not exist within nations, but *between* nations. The rich countries are becoming wealthier, the poor ones more poverty-stricken; at best, the latter remain roughly at their present inadequate economic level. The iron laws of economics and nature seem to hold the same fate in store for them that they once did for the Western working classes. Has the Marxist prophecy that the exploited proletariat would overthrow the bourgeoisie been defeated domestically only to reappear internationally and defeat us on the global plane? Will the poverty-stricken nations of the world, the international proletariat, rise up in revolution against the privileged and wealthy Western countries, the international bourgeoisie? The answer to these questions is probably yes—unless the Western powers, and especially the United States, apply on a global scale the same principle which was so profitable at home, the principle of social justice. . . .  P B ⊘ ⁼ 8 6 1 1

What is missing—and this is *the* essential prerequisite—is a recognition of the extent and urgency of this problem; if the problem is not met, the results will be disastrous to the survival of freedom. There is still not a sufficiently widespread awareness among either political leaders or the American public as a whole. The latter, particularly, enjoying affluence at home, remain blissfully unaware and abysmally ignorant of the problem. Far too frequently, the problem of economic aid is seen only as indicative of American generosity. In short, it is seen not in terms of American security but as charity. . . .

The United States, if it wishes to ensure its survival, *cannot* afford to do less than is demanded by the situation. A Marshall Plan for the underdeveloped world is not just desirable; it is absolutely necessary. And just as governmental intervention in the domestic economy and the redistribution of income laid the foundation for the politically unified and economically prosperous Western nations, so aiding the poor nations can only prove advantageous to the West. Politically, it would help check Communism, which attempts to exploit the hunger and misery of these peoples who comprise two-thirds of the world's population. Economically, it would broaden markets for Western products. . . . Militarily, it is important because many of the strategic goods the United States stockpiles for military purposes (rubber, tin, lead, zinc, chrome, copper, bauxite, magnesium, and uranium) come from these areas. And morally, such a program would live up to all that is decent and fine in the Western tradition.

# Date Due

| JUN 1 8 70 | | | |
|---|---|---|---|
| | | | |
| NOV 15 70 | | | |
| NOV 2 6 84 | | | |
| | | | |
| | | | |
| | | | |
| | | | |
| | | | |
| | | | |
| | | | |
| | | | |
| | | | |
| | | | |
| | | | |
| | | | |

Demco 38-297